HOW TO
MEASURE
MANAGERIAL
PERFORMANCE

How To Measure Managerial Performance

RICHARD S. SLOMA

MACMILLAN PUBLISHING CO., INC.
New York

Collier Macmillan Publishers
London

With special acknowledgment to

Marlin Bree, writer,

for his professional services in developing
portions of this book under the direction of
Richard Sloma

Macmillan Publishing Co., Inc.
866 Third Avenue, New York, N.Y. 10022

Collier Macmillan Canada, Ltd.

Library of Congress Catalog Card Number: 79–55375

Printed in the United States of America

printing number

1   2   3   4   5   6   7   8   9   10

Library of Congress Cataloging in Publication Data

Sloma, Richard S
   How to measure managerial performance.

   Includes index.
   1. Organizational effectiveness. 2. Management--
Evaluation. 3. Performance standards. 4. Management
by objectives. I. Title.
HD58.9.S57   658.4'07'125   79-55375
ISBN 0-02-929240-9

This book is lovingly dedicated to my daughters, Lynn and Karen, who introduced me to the measures of performance of excellence of fatherhood. Maybe one day, if I continue to try very hard, I will favorably measure up to those exceedingly demanding standards. I hope I'm successful; only the very best is worthy of them.

CONTENTS

viii **CONTENTS**

PREFACE

Every stockholder wants to earn a greater return on his investment. Every manager, no matter how large or small the group for which he is responsible, wants his group to perform more effectively. Every subordinate wants to perform as close to his optimum potential as possible. Every employee wants to know where he stands, to know how his performance "shapes up."

Each of these relatively simple needs requires a relatively complex response because each statement embodies a host of qualitative and quantitative comparisons. Finally, a criterion (or set of criteria) must be defined, else there is nothing with which to compare.

Even a cursory review of only a few of the hundreds of management books reveals that these subjects have been dealt with many times. An obstacle to gaining understanding, however, exists because of two (at least) shortcomings of treatment. The first fault of existing literature is the excessive frequency with which specialized treatment is rendered. Too often, one finds that only one function of the firm is dealt with in detail—e.g., marketing or sales operations or controllership. While the treatment presented may be professional, thorough, competent and relevant, it is narrow, restrictive and immobile, in the sense that the knowledge gained cannot be incorporated easily with other specialized books. Thus, an overall, comprehensive understanding can be acquired only by an investment of an inordinate amount of time and study.

Time is the manager's greatest asset, and, therefore, any avenue that conserves time should be traveled.

The second major shortcoming that one encounters when perusing the many books aimed at management and operating control is the inconsistency of definition of strategy, planning, objectives, budgeting, forecasting, reporting and so on. Too often one finds use of the term, "strategy," as a differentiation from "tactic" and then goes on to learn that the author views a "tactic" as an entire division five-year plan.

The principles contained in this book can be applied (and in fact are applied by many firms) to any type of business endeavor. The detailed emphasis, however, is aimed at firms which manufacture products (whether at the raw material, component or finished product level) for industrial and consumer markets. Firms so engaged in multiproduct and/or multiplant operations will find study and application of this book particularly useful.

The need for this book, then, stems from the inadequacy or inconvenience of existing treatments on the one hand, and from the continuing desire of owners, managers, subordinates and employees to enhance their individual position by, first, gaining an understanding of management and operating control principles as they affect all of the major functions of the firm and, second, by *application* of those principles in an increasingly larger framework.

Far too often, one observes that managers fail to implement and practice the principles contained in this book. They fail to pursue discrete measurement and definition of objectives and performance standards.

There is need for this book by many, many incumbent managers. The need exists in the "real world" of business management. There is a need, too, among the thousands of subordinates who seek to become not only managers, but effective managers.

As will be developed later in the book, the effectiveness of the employee's performance is directly related to the extent and consistency with which quantitative approaches are taken to define performance objectives and standards.

Stated very simply, this book, if studied, absorbed and applied, will provide you with a top-level viewpoint from which you will be able to observe all of the firm's major functions, their interrelationships and the common thread of management and operating control. One of the premises of this book is that the reader aspires to be an effective General Manager (or Chief Operating Officer, Chief Executive Officer, President, and so on). To the extent that the premise is valid in your case, you will find this book a valuable reference source. It will be on your desk—not tucked neatly away on the bookshelf.

Consistent and rigorous application of the principles and concepts of this book, particularly if coupled with in-house seminars, will enable your organization to perform at least several levels higher in efficiency and effectiveness.

At a minimum, the managers in your firm will have been made aware of new insights of management techniques.

HOW TO USE
THIS BOOK

I will have failed to achieve *my* most important objective if all you have done is merely to have read this book! We will both achieve our objectives only if you USE this book. How can it be best used? Let's provide some help.

The book can be divided into three unequal sections. The first section, Chapters One through Six, provides a comprehensive overview of the relationship between (a) Alternate Strategy Evaluation, (b) Tactical Planning, and (c) Management Performance—Definition and Measurement. This section seeks to show and tell *how and where management performance measures "fit" into the total scheme of more effective management of the firm.* While it provides a new insight, Section One is NOT a lot of things. It is NOT: a textbook of Business Planning; a comprehensive and exhaustive treatment of functional job responsibilities; a detailed, technical explanation of the content of functional areas of knowledge.

Section Two, Chapters Seven through Twenty Two, is the most voluminous section. While Section One should be read page by page, Section Two is a "dip into" section; a buffet from which you can *select* those objectives and performance measures which are useful to *your* organization at *this* particular time.

Section Two is aimed at two classes of readers: Those who are *initiating* a "No-Nonsense Management" approach; and those who are seeking to *improve and/or expand* management by objective "coverage." There is really very little in this section which is original or unique. You may have seen similar but much more limited treatments elsewhere. The most important feature of this section is that it compiles, in one place for the greatest reference effectiveness, sample objectives and other performance measures for virtually "all" of the major functional areas in a manufacturing organization.

Section Two is the section which should be *"used"* frequently. This book belongs at your right hand on your desk!

Probably the most frequent use of this book will be made by those who, first, have decided that, "Yes, by George! We *will* have objectives to measure management performance!"—and, second, ask, "Where do I begin?" After reading Section One, you begin by skimming Section Two looking for that function in your firm with which you feel *least* comfortable in defining or setting objectives. Then read that chapter and select the half-dozen or so that are most relevant to provide more complete answers to the Background Mangement Data.

Remember! Objectives, once set, are set only for a year or less. They require pruning, adjusting and modification as the needs and aspirations of your firm change—back to Section One. Thus, you can extract the greatest value by making a walk through Section Two several times a year.

After selecting those objectives and measures with which you wish to start your program (or expand your existing program), read Section Three, which consists of only Chapter 23. *Then* begin the negotiating meetings with your subordinates and peers to, first, ensconce the objectives and, second, establish the reporting procedures.

Finally, pick a "launch" date! You're on your way!

P.S. In the various listing of Target Objectives, you will see the letter "N." Wherever you see an "N," you are to insert an appropriate number which is relevant to your firm and your growth pace. Sometimes "N" will be related to time (number of months, a particular date, and so forth); sometimes to dollars; and sometimes to a ratio or percentage.

HOW TO
MEASURE
MANAGERIAL
PERFORMANCE

1

LET'S DESTROY SOME MYTHS—AND IDENTIFY THE NEEDS

Clearing away the accumulated debris is always the best first step in building a new structure. The process of measuring managerial performance is one which has been subjected to misunderstanding and suspicion for years. So, before we begin to unfold the mechanics of measurement of managerial performance, the destruction of some persistent myths will be of help.

The first myth is that "you can't measure managerial judgment." After all, consider the very intangibility of "judgment"; the inextricable interweave with human nature takes it beyond the ken of the calipers. The nuances are simply too ephemeral to be captured, calibrated and calculated.

What utter nonsense! Managerial judgment is measured daily, even hourly, by financial analysts, bankers, creditors, peers, superiors, and subordinates. And even those outside the business community fail to restrain comment—many, indeed, look to publication of such measurements as their prime source of livelihood. The bleeding-heart-do-gooder demigods who cloak themselves in the noble shroud of "consumer advocate" would disappear, as did the Wicked Witch of the East, were it not for their traffic in "measurement" of managerial judgment.

Aside from the abuses, valid measurements of managerial judgment are made every Monday—following Saturday's game. In other words, the effective measure of managerial judgment is the track record of results achieved toward the enhancement of the enduring value of the shareholder's investment.

Nothing is so objective, so deliberate as when the "moving finger" writes

1

numbers on the history of the firm's financial performance. Neither tears, nor adjectives nor adverbs can "wash away" a single datum.

Some of the proponents of this myth don't really intend to be proponents at all. What they really intend to say is, "One cannot quantify the input content of 'judgment' required to successfully perform as a manager." They somehow feel that this statement has greater merit.

Their belief is as unfounded as if they really meant the first version. While the statement is literally true, it has no use. One also cannot quantify the worth of a bachelor's degree or an M.B.A. One also cannot quantify the value of "n" years of "experience"—whatever that is. And so on.

However, an inability to measure or quantify a qualification criterion does not, in turn, support the view that the qualification criterion can, or should, be ignored. But this book is concerned with measurement of managerial performance, not with the epistemological problems encountered in selection of personnel.

The second myth is closely related to a fundamental characteristic of human nature—the need to avoid criticism. The other side of that coin is the desire to hold others accountable—the need to exercise power over other human beings. Because these needs are so basic, expressions of the myth generated by them are pervasive indeed. The myth, as expressed by managers about to implement a management-by-objectives program, is, "The performance of all of my subordinates can indeed be measured; thus, *their* accountability can be quantitatively expressed. Unfortunately, *my* performance measures would involve too many substantial intangibles to be amenable to such close scrutiny."

The demonstration of the myth-content of that statement is amply revealed when (to no one's surprise, really) one hears the exact statement made, in turn, by *that* manager's superior!

It would appear that huge numbers of incumbent managers feel that—as with the self-denial requirements of good physical health—measurements of performance can (and probably *should*) be applied to everyone but them!

The truth is that the managerial performance of EVERY manager in an organization not only can be objectively, equitably and quantitatively measured—it SHOULD be so measured.

A third myth, which has proved to be a formidable obstacle to the installation of an effective management-by-objectives planning and control system, says that effective measurements of performance can only be obtained from the accounting system. Not only can effective measures be obtained from outside of the accounting system, they generally are more valid in the "real-time" sense and in the "statistical" sense.

All accounting systems are conditioned by, among other things, two important factors. The first is that an important goal of any accounting system is to capture "history." It is an after-the-fact process. In other words, the accounting system attempts to express in numbers what *had happened* in the real, physical world. Thus, use of the real-world events, directly, as a source of measurement is not only more economical, it is more accurate because of the second factor which affects the output of the accounting system: " . . . in conformity with generally accepted accounting principles consistently applied . . ." That phrase, seen thousands of times, reveals (surprise to no one who has been engaged in business for any length of time) that accounting is NOT a precise science. It is sometimes generously labeled an art; it is more crudely named at other times.

Thus, output from the accounting system, while perfectly acceptable to the public audit firm, may be not only useless to a management performance measurement program, but actually counterproductive, in that management performance may be inaccurately measured.

All of this is not to say that managerial performance measures should not be drawn from the accounting system and ONLY taken from non–accounting system sources. Rather, it is to say that the "best" array of measures *always* includes a *"blend"* of data, from both outside of and within the accounting system.

In any event, the measures used for performance evaluation should be carefully selected by the general manager, mindful of the extent of the inaccuracy and bias which they respectively contain.

Another myth relative to measurement of managerial performance states that any such program is futile because a manager can "beat the system." If that statement is true, in the particular instance, then the designers and implementers of that program lacked the requisite skill and imagination to design a successful program—one which a manager cannot "beat."

The prime purpose of performance measurement is to provide an objective, impersonal basis for performance evaluation. If the resultant evaluation is faulty, i.e., if the level of performance is actually significantly below that which the measurement system displays, then the evaluation of that performance is obtained from some other, undefined measure.

The obvious solution is to include that "other, undefined" measure within the measurement program. In other words, it is unacceptable to merely bemoan the alleged fact that, really, the measurement program is incomplete and, therefore, it should be abandoned! It is unacceptable because it is ineffective—it does not lead to improvement of the firm's performance.

Sometimes an oft-used myth is expressed, "If we measure managerial performance and particularly if we reward individuals based upon those measurements, the measured managers will mortgage the future to reap the rewards of short-term favorable measures." This myth reveals more about its author than, perhaps, that author truly desires to display. First of all, of course, is the disclosure that the author's management selection criteria leave much to be desired. If the personnel that they have chosen truly are *that* bereft of integrity, fault the *selector; NOT* the selected.

Second, if the measured manager has been given the option of mortgaging the future to reap short-term rewards, the array of performance objectives is extremely faulty. A well thought out, balanced list of objectives would preclude the possibility of such a course of action by the manager being measured. Thus, the "sins" of the program's "father" should not be borne by the program's "son."

And then, there's always the tried-and-*untrue*, "We tried it once and it didn't work." There are three basic problems with that statement. First, one never really knows what "it" means. Did they try a measurement/reward program? Or did they try a well-conceived, professionally developed program?

Not only is the question raised (and answered) concerning the quality of the program attempted, there is also the question of the quality of the implementation of the program.

Finally, there is the problem of the definition of "work." There is NO indication of what the predetermined standard of success was. There is no indication of how far short of expected results the program results were, or even if predetermined standards for success were established.

One is reminded of all too frequently lamentable experience following a running-scared directive to "pay the production planners [and/or buyers, depending on the version] a bonus geared to reduction in inventory." You have heard of that kind of situation, haven't you?

Well, as predictable, the drop in inventory occurred and the bonus payments were made. All well and good, right? *WRONG!* The production planners had immediately, if not sooner, canceled purchase and/or production of as many "A" items as they could identify. The "A" items, recall, are those which register the "highest dollar value/highest usage" among the items in inventory. Because of that action, the drop in inventory dollars did, indeed, occur.

But precisely because of the high usage rate, the lack of availability of the "A" items caused an inability to produce and to ship. Thus, really not surprising at all and in plain words, a lousy program generated lousy results.

So when confronted with the "cop out" of "we tried it once and it didn't work," begin to ask questions. Chances are greatly in your favor that you will uncover something very similar to the "cut inventory" story!

Another myth that drives professional managers up the wall is the attempted escape from accountability that says, "The manager doesn't really exercise control over the external forces that affect his performance ..." and, *ergo*, attempts to measure performance and base rewards on those measurements are exercises in futility and doomed to failure.

How agonizingly often one is confronted with the "external forces beyond my control" excuse for poor results and subsequent claim for personal recognition coupled with a refutation of the "external forces beyond my control" excuse when results are favorable or acceptable.

The truth of the matter is, of course, that in the *broadest* of views there really is no meaningful control which can be exercised by individuals over "macro" events or phenomena, whether social, economic, natural of whatever. But a manager's job description does not saddle him with the responsibility to alter weather patterns, prevent national economic recessions, preclude "wildcat" strikes and so on.

A manager's purview in NOT "macro"—it is "micro." Only a relatively minute, almost miniscule area of managerial responsibility is not amenable to performance measurement. The GNP of the United States, it must not be forgotten, is rapidly approaching one and one-half trillion dollars; a tremendously awesome amount of commerce occurs daily—even hourly. The opportunity to obtain some additional sales volume is bounded only by the creativity and imagination of the manager entrusted with the job.

If the goal is to improve profits, progress can be achieved by expense reduction and improved productivity in addition to increasing sales volume. While the semblance of an argument can be constructed to the effect that, at this particular time and in this particular served market subsegment, additional volume may truly not be available, *there can be absolutely NO rationale to justify inaction in cost/expense reduction efforts*! Thus, while achievement of a total profit improvement goal truly may not be possible within a short time period of measurement, intelligent goal setting would have identified and quantified the subgoals of profit improvement, of cost reduction, expense reduction, productivity improvement and so on, so that the measured manager *can* be held accountable for, say, six of the seven ways to improve profit.

In other words, if the *array* of goals is properly identified and weighted, effective measures of managerial performance within his "micro" world of effective control can indeed be defined. *A 95 percent accountable manager will perform more effectively by far than a ZERO-percent accountable manager.*

The effectiveness with which a managerial performance measurement program is administered is certainly as important as the program itself—perhaps even more so. A well-conceived program, if poorly administered, will result in a counterproductive effort. The most common travesty inflicted on managerial professionalism usually occurs when a measured manager's performance "just misses," i.e., falls short—but just barely—of the bonus threshold. At a time such as that, the evaluator succumbs to the myth that holds, "morale and effectiveness will be enhanced 'if we bend the rules' a little and allow him to earn some bonus. After all, he did try very hard and he came awfully close."

The truth is, of course, just the opposite. A sacrifice of objective professionalism on the altar of subjective "big-daddyism" inflicts irreparable harm on the management organization. None of the measured managers will view their future objectives with any sense of commitment. There is no objective way to "draw the line."

One of the primary principles of effective management, as discussed in my earlier book, *No Nonsense Management* (Macmillan, 1977) will have been violated: "Manage an organization as nature would; show neither malice nor pity." The demonstration of "pity" will be resented, if not immediately, then eventually even by the recipient—his pride will have been damaged; he does not view himself as a "charity case," but obviously his superior does.

The signal will have been transmitted to the peer group: "You don't really have to take the MBO (Management by Objectives) program *all* that seriously, after all! If the boss thinks you deserve a bonus, you'll get it—whether you have crossed the objective threshold or not." Rest assured that the adverse impact will not be diminished in the transmission; in fact, the impact will most probably be magnified.

The consequences are predictable because they are inevitable. The management group will refocus their efforts from goal achievement to demonstration of effort. The stage is set for internal political competition and the actors are in the wings awaiting (and competing for) entrance cues. Unacceptable results will be recorded—but fear not. Any or several of the myths discussed earlier are handy for rationalization of your failure.

And some people just may believe them.

2

MANAGEMENT AND OPERATING CONTROL: AN OVERVIEW

It is helpful, when describing what something is, to define what it is not. Management and Operating Control (MOC), or at least as it is treated in this book, is not concerned with *ownership* control. The many and varied techniques that can be utilized to retain ownership control or to obtain ownership control are dealt with quite adequately elsewhere.

Nor is Financial Planning and Control the essence of Management and Operating Control. Financial Planning and Control is, or should be, primarily concerned with protecting and fairly representing the value of the firm's assets.

In recent years, the view has become more prevalent that the concept of Financial Planning and Control should be broadened to include Managerial Accounting and Reporting. To the extent that such accounting and reporting include features such as responsibility accounting and measurement of variances from predetermined performance standards, they form a part of the array of tools used in Management and Operating Control. They can constitute an important, integral element of Management and Operating Control. But nonetheless, only an element.

The breadth or scope of Management and Operating Control can perhaps be better envisioned if one realizes that required control information flow is not restricted to only the accounting system channels. Management and Operating Control, as a management practice, embraces *all* functions of the firm. In fact, effective MOC utilizes *any and all data* which contribute to measurement of performance so that consistent and regular comparisons can be made.

FIGURE 2-1
Management and Operating
Control (MOC) Process

Statement of
Strategy Elements

} 1/TOP LEVEL

Definition of
Strategy Objectives

Statement of
Plan Elements

} 2/FUNCTIONAL

Definition of
Plan Objectives

Definition of
Performance Standards

Comparisons to
Actual Performance   } 3/SUBFUNCTIONAL

Response Action
to Comparisons

Management and Operating Control centers on the five key sequential areas of activities depicted in Figure 2-1. It is an iterative process. It is a dynamic activity rather than a static, or even episodic activity. This book will deal, in depth, with the first four areas of activity, first, from the top-level viewpoint of the President or the General Manager, and then, in turn, from each functional viewpoint of the firm.

STRATEGY

The strategy of the firm is defined as the complete array of the key (quantitative and qualitative) goals and operating premises upon which the owners have decided. Sometimes, of course, the owner's decisions are formalized by the Board of Directors. The typical stock purchaser, who buys stock in an established, going concern, endorses, by his purchase, the strategy (strategies) of the firm.

This area of activity consists of two subareas. First is the statement of the strategy elements. Second is the definition of those element statements in quantitative terms. There is considerable overlap between these two areas.

Frequently, one or another element statement will be quantitatively defined before all of the element statements are so defined. Conversely, many ongoing firms have documented quantitative strategy goals without first having formally documented the element statement.

One finds strategy element statements in both express and implied forms. Every firm, knowingly or not, behaves according to strategy element statements. The vast majority of firms do not have formal, express documented strategy element statements. The vast preponderance of strategy element statements are only implied. Further, only rarely are strategy objectives defined quantitatively and correctly labeled as strategy objectives.

Strategy formulation and definition activity is performed almost exclusively by owners and/or Board and/or Chief Executive Officers. Only rarely does any one of the functions of the firm provide substantive input. The function most likely to provide strategic input is Marketing; however, the Marketing head is rarely a participant in strategy formulation meetings.

PLANS

For purposes of this book, Plans are defined as any and all documented courses of action in pursuit and supportive of the strategy objectives.

They can exist in and apply to all departments, functions and groups in the firm. They are sometimes referred to, in the literature and in the "real world," as budgets, forecasts, business plans, programs, projects, and so on.

Many of the things said about strategies can also be said about Plans. They exist in all firms. Far more often they are informal rather than formal. Deficiency in formality will adversely affect overall performance in proportion to the size of the organization. That is, the larger the organization the more formality is required to insure effectiveness and consequent achievement of strategic objectives.

The Plan activity area also is subdivided into two major aspects. The first activity area is the Statement of the Plan Elements. The second is the quantification of definitions of the Plan Objectives. Too few firms document Plan Elements and fewer still define Plan Objectives quantitatively.

An important point to make at this time is that most firms suffer from excessive reliance on the accounting system to provide data which will satisfy the requirements of quantitative Plan Objective definition.

Plan Elements and Objectives should embrace both accounting and nonaccounting system data plans. Many Key Plan Elements and Objectives simply cannot be stated in terms of data available through the accounting system.

Finally, all of the major functions of the firm will be discussed in this book at the Functional Plan-level.

Standards

Once the Plan Objectives have been quantitatively defined, Standards of Performance are defined as measurements of minimally acceptable performance which, when attained, will achieve the Plan Objectives.

Standards of Performance for hourly direct labor personnel have long been accepted and implemented. Far too frequently, one finds that managerial personnel have somehow been exempted from similar measurement and scrutiny.

Managerial Standards of Performance can be quantitatively expressed in many ways other than direct output. Target dates, time cycles and market share are only three examples of the many measurements which are relevant and material.

Obviously, Standards of Performance must be expressed in terms of the same "language" as the Objectives. They are the milestones which mark the path toward Objective achievement. They are the criteria against which actual performance will be compared. They are the data points which "track" successful attainment of the Objectives defined earlier.

Performance Standards exist for every major function or activity in the firm. The selection of the specific quantitative value is governed by the gap between the most recently recorded performance and the level defined by the Objective.

The aim of this book, then, is to present arrays of performance standards to enable the reader to effectively implement a sound managerial performance appraisal and planning program.

Comparisons

The comparison of actual performance to the Standards of Performance is the first time in the MOC process when all previous strategizing and planning comes face to face with the "real world." It is also the first time that a shift in time frame of thinking occurs.

In the preceding three steps, the focus of thought is on the future. When comparing actual performance to the Standards of Performance, the relevant time frame is the present—the "now."

Further, time is required to collect the actual data, process it and issue the comparison reports. Thus the reviewer of the results of the comparisons deals with data which occured in the past. The longer the time cycle required for data processing and review, the less useful the result of the comparison as a basis for corrective action.

The comparison step is the point where all of the previous care exercised to state Strategy and Plan Objectives quantitatively bestows rewards. Actual performance data are presented quantitatively: sales dollars, order intake dollars, gross margin dollars, direct labor hours, burden expense dollars,

FIGURE 2-2

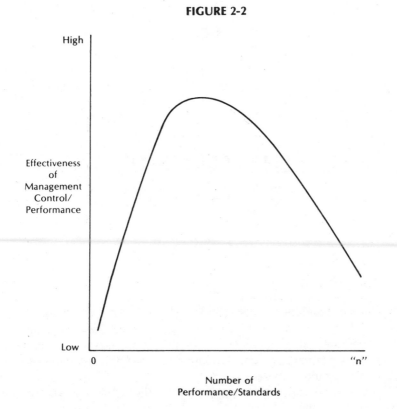

High

Effectiveness
of
Management
Control/
Performance

Low

0   "n"

Number of
Performance/Standards

pounds shipped, number of rejects, and so on. These data can be placed on one side of the balance scale. The matching predetermined Standards of Performance are placed on the other side.

If there are no predetermined Standards of Performance, the balance scale (and evaluative judgment) remains lopsided.

The greater the number of comparisons of Standards of Performance and matching actual data that are available, the more valid the judgment that can be made. Further, the more complete and precise the comparison that can be made, the greater and more valid the operational performance insight that will be obtained.

However, the number of comparisons which can be effectively utilized is governed by the economic law of diminishing marginal utility. Just as the "nth" glass of water will drown a thirsty person, so too will the "nth" comparison consume more time and incur more cost than it is worth. This relationship is depicted in Figure 2-2.

3

THE ELEMENTS
OF STRATEGY

The first step in developing a collection of managerial standards, then, is to begin, as did Alice in Wonderland, at the very beginning. For the managerial team, the necessary starting point is the identification and synthesis of basic wisdom of the organization itself. Suitably developed, this will comprise the organization's elements of strategy.

Surprisingly enough, most companies operate instinctively as if according to certain key elements of strategy. Yet unless these elements are selected, compared, defined and, finally, ascribed, there is very little reason to suspect that any management team continuously can move with fluency from evidence through reasoning to conclusion on any project.

Most companies pay only lip service to corporate planning and basic strategy. They don't get down to the nitty-gritty of what they themselves are really all about. Nor do they spend the required time to define their basic strategy elements or, for that matter, to define the very criteria they use for selecting the unwritten strategy elements they operate upon.

It stands to reason that if you do not have detailed, recorded strategy elements as a model, you really can't come up with quantitative objectives in specific programs because you don't know what strategy you want to implement in the first place.

Formal documentation and identification of strategy elements are important for reasons other than for pure planning. For the diverse corporate structure, they serve as a unifying communications device on what the company is all about. They serve as a corporate memory as well, for though individuals may come and go in the corporation, the corporation itself goes on. All too often, a new arrival or in-house promotion sits like a Christmas tree ornament, only without the tree.

Strategy elements in written form give everyone the basics of what the company is all about and what it wants to do. In this basic area there should be no room whatever for assumption.

Nor should there be guesswork as to the basic goal of the business. It is always related to the improvement of return on investment (ROI). In professional management, the name of the game is usually ROI. That's because management itself is pure function: To turn investment into profit through use. The test comes at the end of the fiscal year, when shareholders look at the bottom line to see what management has performed.

Though management, especially at the functional levels, usefully thinks of performance in terms of goals, objectives, markets or even sales volume, rather than assets employed, the shareholder thinks only about the latter and often has little interest in sales or profits per se. The total picture for the stockholder is there on the bottom line: ROI. ROI determines whether the investment will continue and whether the stock will go up or down. And if you are also wondering, whether the team at the top will survive for long.

ROI can be financial or psychological. For example, if you are the owner of a small business, you are certainly entitled by virtue of your position to define ROI either way, or even as a blend of both. You may, for example, derive psychological income from intentionally keeping a "loss" product in the line because you designed it. Or you may keep extra people on the payroll even though they do not perform up to acceptable standards. The amount of psychological ROI derived is the exact difference between what is acceptable in this example and what the business would generate if it were professionally managed for maximum ROI. Any gap, or shortfall, between these two standards is the exact measure of the dollar value of psychic income an owner enjoys.

While an owner is entitled to take home all the tax-free psychic income as is his or her expressed preference, this person is equally entitled to poverty, if he or she so desires. The point is, each should recognize the situation as it actually is, and then make a choice.

And that's part of the point of this book. We assume most managements and owners have an implied preference for ROI maximization. We also assume that most managements will pursue goals of ROI enhancement if they know the clear paths to follow and, furthermore, will define the position of the firm so that there is a clear indication to everyone on which way to go. It is also assumed that management will insist, by planning techniques, on taking a purposeful, willful position relating to expected, accepted ROI levels.

The purpose of this chapter is not to duplicate other, more detailed presentations of defining strategy elements, nor even to present a lengthy discourse on why they are universally necessary. But we do want to emphasize that as a necessary condition to determine performance standards that strategy elements recording and analysis is not only a necessary step, but it is a *preliminary* step. Furthermore, it should occur in the sequence as presented in this book.

At the end of this chapter, as in other chapters which will follow, are presented elements which begin to comprise performance standards as a "checklist." These are the "models" upon which each individual organization can build its own standards. These are the *crucial* elements which must be addressed in each firm—even if the response is, "we have no strategy element in this area for our firm."

It is important to put each response *on paper* so that it is recorded, in black and white, for all to see. It's also important not to make polarity judgments about them at this time; that is, to attempt to determine whether they are, per se, good or bad. Instead, just try to capture your answer as succinctly as possible, and try to treat each for what it is, doing so with candor and honesty. There is no room whatever for wishful thinking here: Remember that Mickey Rooney, in his heart of hearts, may strongly strategize a plan to be 6 feet, 4 inches tall. But the odds are he won't make it.

STRATEGY ELEMENT CONSIDERATIONS

As you begin to document your strategy element statements based on the "checklist," your goal should be consistency, rather than conciliatory.

Here are several considerations to make regarding each element:

Profit

What people think they know about a firm may not be true until it is documented and tested. There is but one test for professional performance, and that is ROI. Incidentally, in the development of this point of the basic strategy elements, there will usually be an inverse proportion between the amount of input from the treasurer's department and the error content in profit planning below that which can realistically be done. In other words, treasurers at the crap table always bet you'll never roll the eight.

Products

Consider that it is better to survive with a few winners than to go into involuntary bankruptcy through product proliferation.

Market Scope

It's better to serve one market very well than to fail at many. Before deciding to develop new products for new markets, satisfy yourself that the geographic expansion of your present market served may not offer greater rewards.

Market Posture

There is often a tradeoff in this regard between market share and ROI. Consider what it will cost to gain the extra percent of market share; it may not be worth the extra cost. Though the best of all worlds is to be a big fish in a big pond, there's not room for all of the fish to be big in little ponds. Sometimes small, then, is beautiful—especially for ROI enhancement.

A firm's market posture should be a conscious, intentional decision, not one resulting essentially from default. There is nothing wrong in purposefully adopting the posture of a follower rather than that of a leader. Some firms have done very well over the years without incurring the cost of a pioneering effort. The point is to determine in advance what you want to be, so that the right inferences can be made which will lead you to the specific programs you want—with the right kind of posture.

Technical Spectrum

Two questions: First, where are you in terms of engineering content, and, second, where *should* you be in terms of the market and the requirements of the market? And, is there a high or a low engineering content in your product?

Inferences from this line of inquiry are several: If you are in the low end, the prospects for either successful product development in a high technical area or a successful acquisition of such a firm are extremely doubtful. Any acquisition is, after all, measured much like a marriage: not by the original ceremony, but by the silver jubilee.

And, generally speaking, the higher the engineering content in the product, the lower should be your finished goods inventory. For example, one of the highest technical products in the United States is the moonshot rocket, and there are not a lot of those around. The converse also is true: The *lower* the engineering content, the more dependent you are upon skillful deployment of working captial. If you are selling common nuts and bolts, then, you had better have excellent distribution and close control of your accounts receivable.

Long Term/Short Term

By the planning process, beginning with strategy elements, a firm can insist on taking a conscious, purposeful position. Determined here, for example, are the long-term goals for which strategy elements must first be drawn. But one factor here must be remembered: in planning for the future, don't extrapolate as if the future were simply the same as the past continued. Usually, the future involves one or more abrupt, sharp transitions from a purely linear development.

Important also in this element is to consider the planning base for the long term. If you're going to build, then consider the example of the skyscraper: The taller the building, the deeper the foundation you need for stability.

**STRATEGY
ELEMENTS
CHECKLIST**

—PROFIT (OR NONPROFIT)

—PRODUCTS (OR SERVICES)

—MARKET SCOPE (GEOGRAPHIC)

—MARKET POSTURE
  • Leader?
  • Follower?

—TECHNOLOGICAL SPECTRUM POSITION
  • High?
  • Low?

—MARKET POSITION:
  • Raw material
  • Component
  • Product
  • Reseller (wholesale/retail)?

—LONG-TERM (VS. SHORT-TERM)

—PUBLIC (OR PRIVATE)

—CHANNELS:
  • Contract?
  • Direct?
  • OEM?
  • Distributor?
  • Or all of the above?

4

ORGANIZING STRATEGY OBJECTIVES

Strategy objectives are derived from strategy elements. Because the elements are almost always qualitative, they are not amenable to measurement and quantitative analysis. The aim of strategy elements is to put the goals of the owners into language. The objectives are the text from which we can extract and further define quantitative measures which will provide the milestones with which to track our progress toward the fulfillment of the defined elements.

While there is a close correlation between the elements and the objectives of strategy, it is well to keep in mind that strategy elements are probably the least productive area in which to attempt to apply quantitative techniques.

For example, we may want to say that, as a strategy element, we want to become the market dominator. In itself, this is sufficient as a strategy element so that when it is communicated, the officer management group can begin to develop plans which target at specific growth patterns. Knowing that the owners want to achieve a dominant market position, the management group then can begin to construct the specific quantitative plans and programs such that the corporation's market share can progress from the 20 percent share now held to, say, 55 percent.

It is from these *planned* programs that inferences can be made affecting other functions of the firm. For example, we can insure that Operations has sufficient plant capacity to economically produce a number of units to achieve the targeted share objectives. Further we can anticipate that an adequate distribution system will be in place to carry the product to the customer in sufficient quantity and at an appropriate cost so that the achievement of dominant market share does not conflict with the strategy of maximizing investment.

Certainly, a keystone purpose of determining strategy objectives is to communicate the wishes of the owners and the management group throughout the organization: to provide everyone with the basic guidelines which they sorely need to ensure that the plans and the programs that are developed are consistent with the aims of the owners. All too often in business, the wishes of the owners are available only indirectly and by implication. For instance, it is conceivable that specific personnel changes contemplated by line management, which they believe to be consistent with their perception of what they think the owners want, are sorely off course. One day, these managers awaken to find that the owners have decided against this personnel action and are amazed that management did not understand what was in their heart of hearts—despite the fact that the owner's wish was heretofore *uncommunicated*. What this means, sometimes, is that a fair-haired "favorite" could be up for termination, entirely consistent with a communicated strategy element, but have that termination denied because of a previously uncommunicated strategy element. That uncommunicated strategy element, incidentally, might be, "I want to be Santa Claus," to which the owners are perfectly entitled.

Communication is a prime goal of all business planning. It can be significantly enhanced by quantifying objectives within the strategy element statements. In other words, the more guidance and especially the more specific quantitative guidance that can be given to line management, the more expansive and relevant can be their planned programs.

The owners, acting through the board and probably in consultation with line management, should attempt to document as complete a list of strategy objectives as practical. An important feature to keep in mind is that while strategy objectives must eventually be feasible and practical there is absolutely no need to try to anticipate the results to be achieved toward these objectives.

By analogy, the most useless sales forecast in a five-year profit plan is one which attempts to forecast levels of production output capability. The professional approach is actually a "yo-yo" affair, just as is the preparation of a profit plan. The owners may wish to have a dominant market share of 90 percent and it well may be the case that line management, apprised of this strategy objective, may well respond that in the foreseeable future 55 percent is the most that may be obtained.

Assuming that line management has tried to inject an element of conservatism, the owners and management then negotiate to explore the realism of each other's position. The net result can very well be a market share strategy objective of 58 percent.

Similarly, the treatment of all other objectives can be handled in an open, back-and-forth manner until a workable end result can be obtained. Line management has a voice (really, they have an obligation) in the evaluation of strategy objectives. The posture of the owners should be aggressive, and the burden of proof for acceptance of something less than what the owners identify should rest properly with the line management.

There are, of course, a number of factors which will enter into the negotiation process. Some of these considerations are the effect the end results will have on the firm's financials. Eventually, the most effective communication tool is an abbreviated set of pro forma financial statements. The three basic statements are, of course, Profit and Loss (PL), Balance Sheet, and Cash Flow.

The priority of importance of these three statements will vary in each individual situation depending on the needs of the organization and the strategy elements expressed by the owners. For example, if a strategy element is "milk the company," or "bail the company out of bankruptcy," then clearly the cash flow statements are the focal point for concerted management attention.

But if the situation is a publicly held corporation with relatively widespread holdings, the strategy element might be to maximize market price, in which case earnings per share tend to dominate the thinking and to focus management's attention on the PL.

STRATEGY OBJECTIVES CONSIDERATIONS

Financial
The biggest mistake that can be made at this point in the management process is the preparation of and reliance on only *one* set of financials. In other words, it is well to develop alternate scenarios to quantify optimistic and pessimistic results in addition to "realistic" results. In this way, you know you will have included the most likely results that will occur. Test your scenarios for acceptability and conformance with not only strategy objectives but the strategy elements as well. Take your time: The financials are the flight plan for your growth activity.

Strategies
Managements sometimes get blind spots when it comes to how big a market need they actually foresee. To maximize profits, consider a strategic point of view to trade off maybe three or four points of market share by incremental price increases, changed methods of distribution or modified distribution. Reconsider regionally served markets; it really may not pay for a firm in

Minneapolis, for example, to serve Florida with goods manufactured in Minneapolis. Sometimes it is actually better to retreat three or four points on the market share rather than to go full-bore for all-out expansion. Sometimes "less" market share can very well be "more."

Strategy objectives should also take into account a growing burden of governmental regulatory intrusion. There have been many dilutive tendencies inherent in ill-conceived and unachievable social goals foisted on the shoulders of management by governmental fiat. One of the biggest contributors to our woes, to say nothing of our nation's lack of productivity growth, has been the mountains of regulations from our overly ambitious and burgeoning bureaucracy that has practically overwhelmed American industry's ability to respond. Consider that every seventeen minutes of every working day a new regulation is issued which further constrains, restricts or otherwise inhibits opportunity for corporate growth.

In the popular polls over the past several decades, a slipping confidence in America's business management system has been expressed. Some of the slippage is due to the "bad press" which business receives from some of the media. But part of the slippage is due to the management's overanalytical and sometimes confused orientation, in part attributable to lack of well-defined and widely understood objectives. The net result is that managers lack dedication to profits and steady, long-term real growth; we are overly preoccupied with wide-eyed, faddish movements and theories. As such, we have abdicated a big chunk of our own responsibility. So after years of nonsense, we (and shareholders) are ready for a no-nonsense approach once more.

The hard business world facts of life are, after all, that one gets no rewards for theory or social responsiveness as intoned by the wild-eyed liberals and manipulators of the past several decades. One gets rewards only for results, notably ROI, which is the name of the management game.

A basic problem with many managements lies not so much in motivation as in understanding what objectives they are to follow. Remember that the objectives of the "robber barons" of the nineteenth century may have been socially reprehensible, but at least they were clearly defined, well understood and vigorously pursued.

The driving motivation force needs, really, only to be redirected toward "the bottom line."

**STRATEGY
OBJECTIVES
CHECKLIST**

—FINANCIAL STATEMENT EMPHASIS:

- P&L
- Balance Sheet
- Cash Flow

—STRATEGIES VARY ACCORDING TO CHANGING:

- Market Needs
- Political Developments
- General Economic Conditions

5

PLAN STATEMENTS

As a general manager, your primary responsibility is to implement the strategy which has been defined for the firm. It is up to you to translate strategy statements into near-term or short-term objectives which must be achieved by your organization.

But before you can quantify the objectives that must be achieved, you must develop the statements of plans which will lead to objective definition and selection. The most critical statements which can be made focus on control and the reasonability of achievement. While you will depend in part on data from financial or accounting reporting systems, you must look beyond those data for performance measures.

Before entering into the detail of the construction of plan statements, let's look first at the conceptual framework within which the statements should be formulated. For ease of reference, as well as for clarity, this conceptual framework probably can best be stated in the form of fourteen planning rules:

1. *Organizational Suitability Rule:* All controls should reflect the organization's *planned* structure.
2. *Planned Congruence Rule:* All controls must conform with the structure and the character of the plans.
3. *Forewarning Control Rule:* Controls must be set up to warn of future unfavorable deviations from plans.
4. *Assurance of Objectives Rule:* Controls should accomplish specific

23

objectives by early detection of deviations from plan so that management can take corrective action early.

5. *Efficiency of Control Rule:* The only efficient controls are those which allow detection of deviations and make corrective action possible.
6. *Effective Standards Rule:* Control is possible only when quantitative, measurable and relevant standards are in place and operational.
7. *Strategic Controls Rule:* Effective controlling requires attention to those strategic factors which are key to the appraisal of performance.
8. *Variance Rule:* Control efficiency is maximized when attention is focused primarily on significant variances.
9. *Flexibility of Controls Rule:* Controls should always have enough flexibility to be effective even when performance falters. Remember that plans don't fail—people do.
10. *Review Rule:* The performance areas governed by the control system must be reported and reviewed periodically.
11. *Control Responsibility Rule:* Those who use controls should also be involved in their development (participative management).
12. *Accountability Control Rule:* Each manager must be held individually accountable for results.
13. *Rule of Managerial Action:* Controls are useful only if followed by managerial action to correct deviations in plans through planning, organizing, staffing and directing.
14. *Organizational Control Rule:* Control of an organization is best achieved through attention to the quality of up-and-coming managers.

Planning statements will eventually be translated into planning objectives. But the time to build in the control and the reporting system is that time in which the plan statements are first formulated. It is during this formulation that the *spirit* of the plan statements is best known.

As we shall see in the next chapter, the plan objectives are really a series of *numbers*. But the thought process of plan statement formulation should embrace consideration of the control that may be needed to ensure proper monitoring of the resultant objectives.

The following list of ten criteria for evaluation of the adequacy and the effectiveness of governing control systems should be borne in mind as the rules are applied in the planning statement definition process:

1. Is it simple? Controls should be no more elaborate than they have to be to first detect, and then correct, significant deviations from plans. A good

guide for control design is to test to see if significant deviations crop up.

2. Is it positive? Controls are brought into place not so much to keep things from happening as to make certain the right things happen at the right times. Obtaining results is the highest purpose of controls.

3. Is it decisive? Merely setting up a control is no guarantee it will work. Control should not end with detection, but only when the performance fault is eliminated.

4. Do plans and controls go together? A plan that does not contain controls to make it happen is not a likely candidate for success.

5. Is responsibility for execution combined with control? A person responsible to get a job done should also have sufficient authority to exercise the necessary controls. When controls and responsibility are dovetailed, coordination is simplified and many problems are avoided.

6. Is control focused on variance? When a variance has been made from standards, then control is fairly easy to determine and to apply. Primary attention here should be made to the definition and the detection of variances.

7. Is control concentrated at "key" points? If it is not possible to control entire processes throughout their entire cycle, then control must be established at points where change may occur.

8. Are controls located advantageously? Controls should not strain an organizational relationship, for they are most effective when they and the organization are compatible.

9. Does the control have sufficient time span to remain effective? Controls should be maintained in place and operational throughout the duration of the plan.

10. Is control in the hands of qualified personnel? Only managers who are qualified to use control should be given control. But controls should match the expected performance of the managers who use them.

Effective control, while not totally dependent upon accounting system or financial system reporting, must rely heavily on data emanating from these two sources. Again, a conceptual framework is very useful to develop the design of the financial reporting system that will (or should be) developed and implemented to support the planning and the execution by management. The key factors to consider are:

Key Factors	*Performance Payoff*
1. Determination of economic and technical characteristics of the organization.	Assures that unique and important organizational characteristics are integrated in the strategic planning process.

2. Establishment of customer demands in regard to the company's product line, production capability and competition.

Provides a common catalyst for the integrated planning of production facilities, research and development, long-range financing and sales forecasting. It also establishes a solid basis for program budgeting, profit planning and operations budgeting.

3. Analysis of pure corporate policy and strategic planning factors.

Generates a deep understanding of the organization as well as its environment. Forms a more intimate basis for management decisions at all levels.

4. A planning time span of adequate length; five-year or other comparable operating cycle.

Permits measurement of factors including technical, economic or environmental changes against such a time span. In turn, this can help in taking timely action.

5. Levels of management vertically integrated for effective planning coordination.

Aligns involvement and cooperation vertically throughout the management structure according to strategy guidelines and corporate policy set by executive management. Establishes a success criteria.

6. Evaluation criteria to determine the degree of success in attaining corporate objectives.

Establishes the success criteria for the evaluation of the accomplishment of corporate strategies through achievement of specific objectives.

7. Analyzing past, present and possible future changes in the environment and in society.

Provides an opportunity to study and plan for governmental controls, environmental impact studies, international trade constraints and other factors, including shortages of materials.

8. Investigation of risks involved in various alternatives.	Allows controlled contingency planning.
9. Establishment of guidelines for the acquisition, development and performance of executives.	Provides clearly defined criteria for the evaluation of executive performance. Personnel are aware of corporate expectations.

Only in rare instances does a manager have the opportunity to design a financial reporting and control system from scratch. Invariably, there is some kind of financial reporting and control system in place. But how does a general manager evaluate the adequacy of the existing financial reporting and control system? Just as a doctor observes a patient and makes inferences from symptoms, so, too, should a business "doctor" view his other financial reporting and control system. By the same method, one can move through the analysis from recognition features to areas for improvement. A list of these recognition features and suggested improvement opportunities is shown below:

Recognition Features	*Improvement Opportunities*
1. No formal organizational structure, or an existing structure which is out-of-date and does not reflect existing lines of reporting authority	Develop and publish current organizational charts to clearly define lines of reporting and who's responsible for what. This charting is basic to any effective organization's communications channels and informal pecking order. Effective two-way communications is dependent upon defined channels. Such channels usually don't exist without published organizational charts religiously maintained and always up to date.
2. Planning guides, policy and/or procedural manuals that are no longer current	Management should review and update plans, policies and procedures, and all corporate communications devices. A gap in this communications area shows up somewhere as a gap in documented and communicated

policy, procedures or planning—and usually expensively.

3. Preparation of the budget and corporate planning activities are carried out once a year, accompanied by much complaining and foot-dragging. The entire event is a traumatic experience, if not an outright imposition, on management, which does all it can to do as little as possible.

Planning activities, like creative thinking, should be a continuous process that occurs routinely throughout the year. New trends should be incorporated into the process as needed and new thinking regularly encouraged and utilized. Overall, these planning activities should not be one-shot events, for any single, sole effort to get together to "plan" is not likely to produce spectacular results. Management attitudes toward planning ought to be the same as toward breathing: It's better when it continues on a regular basis. Insistence on quarterly reforecasts smooths the learning curve.

4. The results of the financial reporting system don't match up with what should be happening based on organizational accountability.

Compare what is happening with what should be happening. This analysis will pinpoint the way to needed changes, either for systems or for management.

5. Specific responsibilities for organizational planning have not been formally assigned to specific people or have been fobbed off to untrained staff personnel.

Planning should be the responsibility of line management with specific assignments who work within a system of procedures and deadlines. Otherwise, planning has little real chance of success and will, in fact, usually continue to be an absurd abstraction.

6. Management spends much of its time "firefighting" or otherwise reacting to unexpected problems.

Most "problems" faced by organizations should have been anticipated long in advance by effective planning. Management should have in hand "alternatives" based on prior analysis. Carefully developed strategies and plans should provide, a priori, the basis for answers to most economic, operational, technical or personnel "firefights" faced by management.

7. Top management takes part actively in daily operations and makes decisions for operational levels.

By not delegating responsibility, top management does everyone else's job but its own. Sometimes a manager with a specific background, such as engineering for example, will want to continue a strong involvement in that field. But top management must confine itself to those areas of top management—or return to those areas in which it obviously feels most comfortable.

8. Top management positions or high-level promotions are not made from within but from "outside" recruiting.

The best organization is a vibrant one in which every top spot is virtually encircled by those who would compete for advancement. A lack in this vital area indicates a need for planning or training to have advancement from within—or a planned for, but massive, "new blood" transfusion from without. An organization's greatest resource is utimately its human resource, and in depth.

9. High levels of employee or supervisory turnover in any one department. Also, high absenteeism rates, interdepartmental bickering and infighting. Excessive overtime.

These behaviors are symptomatic of managerial problems which should be fully investigated. Chances are that other problems will be uncovered which have been "masked" or otherwise not yet become apparent. Check especially to determine if corporate policies, guidelines and other main elements of corporate wisdom are in place and are working. Lack of such communication, poorly prepared documents or withholding of such information can be a source of many problems.

10. Outside consultants, training or professional services are not made use of even when they have been budgeted for and are considered appropriate.

Such professional services often can provide an organization with the appropriate disciplines it needs on a timely basis to identify and help solve problems. Moreover, they can often identify the *symptoms* of problems. Though various managerial groups may claim they are "too busy" or other such nonsense, a timely check may well uncover serious weaknesses within the group which secretly fears "disclosure" by an outside consultant.

The information base from which plan statements can be developed should include, of course, all of the major functional areas of the firm. See below. To prematurely attempt to formulate each meaningful plan statement without regard to this information base will result in immature and probably suboptimal plan objectives.

Table 5-1

**PLAN STATEMENT
INFORMATION BASE**

1. Markets

Market share:
  • ours
  • our competitors'
Total market size:

Factors determining market:
- size
- nature

Sales projections or forecasts:

2. Marketing & Distribution

Methods:
- ours
- competitors'

Effectiveness of methods
employed:
- ours
- competitors'

Marketing support:
- advertising
- promotion
- technical services
- public relations
- communications

Effectiveness of marketing support:
- advertising
- promotion
- technical services
- public relations
- communications

Customer service adequacy
- delivery performance
- ours
- competitors'
- effectiveness of salespeople

Sales performance:
- in comparison with forecast or
  budget
- incoming orders
- new account analysis
- lost account analysis

- lost orders analysis
- return sales analysis
- customer complaint analysis

Profitability:
- type of distribution
- profiles of customers
- geographical areas

Marketing and distributing
expense control:

Dealer organization:
- soundness
- profitability
- knowledge

Customer inventory analysis:

Reciprocal sales:

3. Products

Product line:

Product line stage:
- growth/decline
- trend/cycle

Coverage provided:

Product of competitor:
- direct evaluation
- evaluation of substitutes

Specifications vs. quality:

Performance in response to
customer needs:

New products:

Product improvements:

Profitability (or lack of it):

Product feedback:
- customers
- salespeople

Warranty/guarantee Analysis:

Value/cost relationship to product design:

4. Prices

Pricing structure:
- ours
- competitors'

Price deviations:

Quantity (volume) changes impacting on:
- price
- quality
- other factors

5. Facilities & Methods

Physical Characteristics of existing plant:

Utilization and capacity:

Status of technology:

Deficiencies and opportunities:
- problems of quality
- inefficiency of production
- imbalances in production facilities

Requests and opportunities for capital expenditures:

Capital expenditures:
- project control
- project follow-up

Maintenance costs:

Production methods:
- resulting from past improvements
- possibility for improvements

6. Physical Production Planning & Inventories

Sales order status

Purchase order status

Economic lot size:
- purchasing
- purchasing points

Vendor performance

Production schedule

Production cycle lead-time

Labor schedule & machine loading

Inventory positions including turnover

7. Manufacturing Costs

Costs (present & past) of:
- products
- components
- packaging
- departments
- cost divisions
- processes

Standards and deviations:
- standard conformance
- deviation causes
- deviation trends

Cost types:
- direct
- programmed
- periodic

Results of make/buy/study:

Productivity of labor:
- indirect
- direct
- overtime
- extra costs

Rework and reject costs:

Space:
- idle
- empty

Manufacturing lot sizes:

Effects of cost reductions:

8. Research & Development
Opportunities for Research

Goals and effort
Proposal and evaluation:
- new materials
- new products
- product improvements
- process improvements

Projects:
- technical status
- technical costs

Personnel:
- experience
- qualifications

Scientific support:

Value of Previous Research to the company:

Keeping informed about current discoveries and industry advances:

9. Financial

Working capital and cash:
- positions
- forecasts
- analyses

Current ratios:

Utilization of line of credit:

Investment opportunities:
- temporary

Analysis of inventory investment:

Accounts receivable:
- turnover
- collection problems
- age

Debt to equity status:

Sufficient reserves:

Investigation of surplus:

Spending requirements:
- Long-term
- Short-term

Capital:
- Sources
- Availability

Changes in the money market:

Stock:
- Prices
- P/E trends
- Opinions of analysts
- Changes in ownership

Lease obligations:

Sufficient insurance coverage:

Contingent obligations such as
financial guarantees:

Taxes:

Internal accounting control:

10. Employees

Organizational structure:
- duties
- responsibilities

Executives:
- value
- continuity
- succession
- compensation and benefits

Labor:
- skills
- ages
- number of employees
- turnover
- morale
- union grievances

- availability
- vacancies
- severance investigation

Employee suggestions:

11. General

Information on basis of balance
sheet, profit and loss, and
cash-flow:
- ours
- theirs

Break-even point:

Budget:

Long-range plans:

Return on investment:

Variations from:
- budgets
- plans
- standards

Corporate objectives:

Relationships:
- community
- corporate

External forces:
- labor
- taxes
- economic conditions
- political

It will be a rare situation, indeed, when a newly arrived manager will find complete and thorough data in this information base. Nevertheless, it is important to analyze and examine the adequacies of the available data base to verify that none of the really key areas are void. If they are, then the immediate action should be to fill those gaps prior to beginning the task of formulating plan statements.

The Organizational Accountability Matrix (Figure 5-1) presents the primary and principal interrelationships that exist between management influence and control over the various balance sheet and profit and loss statements recording lines. It is presented more as a suggestive than as an exhaustive table. It is recommended that you develop a similar table for your organization. It will aid the general manager in understanding the complete overview of his firm and will aid the functional managers in that they will be more aware of the specific planning statement tasks which they face.

Plan statements cannot really be relevant and effective for a particular firm unless they somehow accommodate, and thereby take into account, gross economic behavior.

The most effective micro-economic planning, while very precise, can be totally irrelevant and unachievable if the macro-economic environment is misunderstood. To ensure relevancy in your plan statement formulation, you must properly consider the exogenous variables which may impact your firm. Two tables, 5-2 and 5-3, may provide some suggested approaches.

Clearly, not all of these indicators will be useful in all firms; equally clearly, there are some indicators not listed on the tables which may be very relevant to your particular firm.

A common mistake in business planning is made when the planner looks for a cause-and-effect relationship between the indicator and his firm's business performance.

For suggested planning, all that is really needed is a predictable and high correlation coefficient between the indicator and the firm's performance. For example, if your firm is in the construction industry, a useful indicator may well be the sales of drafting paper to architectural firms. The presumption is that the more drafting paper that architectural firms use the more business they are quoting on, and therefore, the higher the level of business opportunity that may be available to your firm.

One of the major problems one faces when formulating plan statements is to know who should be responsible for definition of plan statements in various functional areas. This is particularly troublesome when the manager is facing the task of initiating the planning process.

Table 5-4 is provided to suggest a start-point for the manager who faces that problem. Clearly, it will need to be tailored to your individual firm. But it is felt that the *format* suggested will prove to be more valuable than the specific content shown in this table.

Probably the most valuable "secret" to defining meaningful plan statements is the satisfactory completion of the prerequisite step of knowing how

FIGURE 5-1
Organizational Accountability Matrix

	Sales	Finished goods inventory	Work in progress inventory	Raw Materials inventory	Production requirements	Labor needs	Material requirements	Manufacturing costs (indirect)	Expenses — nonfactory depts.
Sales management	●				●				
Finished goods inventory management					●				
Work in process inventory management					●				
Raw materials inventory management					●		●		
PRODUCTION MANAGEMENT									
Production requirements (units)	●	●	●	●	●		●	●	
Direct labor requirements					●				
Direct material requirements				●					
Indirect manufacturing expenses					●				
OPERATING MANAGEMENT									
Nonfactory Depts. expense									
Capital improvements									
Costs of goods manufactured			●		●				
Costs of Sales	●	●							
Purchases							●		
Other income & expense									
Prepaid expenses & accruals								●	●
FINANCIAL GENERAL MANAGEMENT Accounts Payable							●	●	
Payroll						●		●	●
Accounts Receivable	●								
Cash									
Balance Sheet		●	●	●					
Loans Payable									
P & L	●							●	●

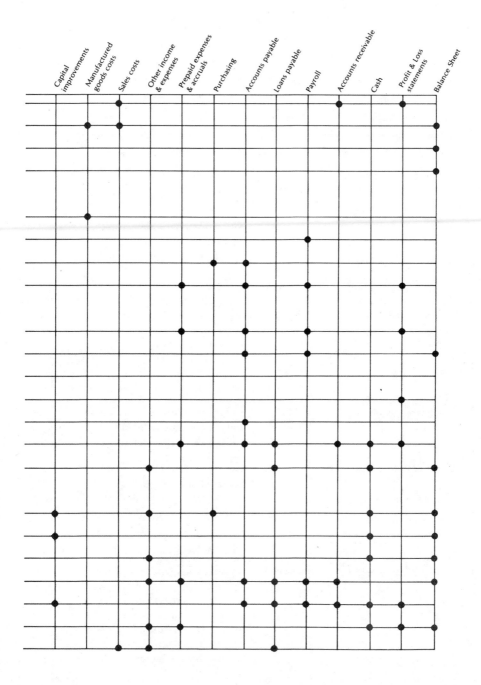

Table 5-2

AVAILABLE ECONOMIC INDICATORS
USEFUL FOR FORECASTING

Economic Indicators	*Indicator Sources*
Lead series:	
Average hours worked (manufacturing)	U.S. Dept. of Labor, Bureau of Labor Statistics
Industrial building contracts	F.W. Dodge: construction contracts awarded for commercial and industrial buildings
National Bureau of Economic Research Lead Indicator Series	National Bureau of Economic Research
Consumption indicators	Mass media, other communciations which report on changes in the relationship of consumption expenditures to total personal income
Surveys showing plans for future action:	
Manufacturing employment	U.S. Dept. of Labor, Area Labor Market Trends
Consumer expenditures	The Federal Reserve Board, Survey Research Center, University of Michigan
Plant & equipment: business expenditures	NICB Capital Appropriations Survey, McGraw-Hill, Securities and Exchange Commission, and the U.S Dept. of Commerce
Government expenditures	President of the United States' January budget report
Opinions, expectations and trends:	
Business management	Dun's Review and Modern Industry, Fortune Magazine and Business Week
Banking management	American Bankers' Association
Economists	Reports of various forecasting conferences of economists, National Association of Business Economists, American Economic Assn. and NICB — Business Outlook

Dominant influences:

Profit prospects	National and local business press articles and reports
Inventory demands	U.S. Dept. of Commerce
Business psychological influences	Business news and reports; analysis of the stock markets

Favorable and unfavorable factors:

Federal Reserve Policy	Communications about the Federal Reserve, either directly or through periodicals and newspapers
Retail sales	U.S. Dept. of Commerce reports, media reports
Manufacturing new orders, backlogs	U.S. Dept. of Commerce reports or various business press articles, national newspapers and magazines
Residential construction	U.S. Dept. of Commerce, specialty publications and metropolitan daily newspapers' business pages
Manufacturing employment trends	U.S. Dept. of Commerce figures, various news and periodical reports
Consumer durable sales	The Federal Reserve Bulletin, various periodicals and publications
Manufacturing capital expenditures	U.S. Dept. of Commerce, business press figures

Recurring trends and cycles:

Textiles	Business press, trade publications
Capital goods	U.S. Dept. of Commerce
Consumer credit	Federal Reserve Bulletin, various national press reports

Critical Levels:

Sales and backlogs vs. inventories	U.S. Dept. of Commerce, various specialty press reports
Capacity vs. production levels	Wharton School of Finance and Commerce's research reports, U.S. Dept. of Commerce

Consumer credit vs. disposable income	Federal Reserve Bulletin, various reports in national business press
Change rates: Production: total, durables and nondurables	Federal Reserve Board
Disposable income levels	U.S. Dept. of Commerce

Table 5-3

BUSINESS CYCLE INDICATORS
AND THEIR LEAD/LAG TIMES

Indicators	Median Lead (−) or Lag (+) in Months	
	Peak	Trough
Leading group		
Employment		
Manufacturing average workweek	−5	−4.5
Manufacturing gross accession rate	−10	−4
Manufacturing layoff rates, inverted	−9	−7
New Investments		
Commercial and industrial building contracts	−9	−1.5
Durable goods new orders	−6	−2
Starts of housing	−14	−5
Number of business net changes	−3	−5
Production		
Gross National Product (current prices)	+ .5	−1
Gross National Product (constant prices)	0	−3
Industrial production index	0	−1
Income and Trade		
Sales by retail stores	+2.5	− .5
Personal income	+1	−2
Bank debits (outside NYC)	+1.5	−3

Stock, Profits and Business Failures		
Common stock price index	−4	−5
Corporate profits (after taxes)	−4	−2
Business failures, liabilities	−7	−7
Wholesale Prices		
Wholesale prices, excluding farm products & foods	+1	+1
Inventory Investment and Sensitive Commodity Prices		
Business inventory changes	−17.5	−5.5
Industrial materials (spot market price index)	−7.5	0
Coinciding Groups		
Employment and unemployment:		
1. Nonagricultural employment	0	0
2. Unemployment rate	−4	+1.5
Lagging Group		
Manufacturing wage and salary cost (per unit of output)	+6.5	0
Consumer's installment debt (end of month)	+5.5	+3.5
Bank interest rates on business loans (last month of quarter)	+5	+5
Plant and equipment expenditures	+1	+2
Manufacturing inventories (book value, end of month)	+1.5	+3.5

to frame the right question. It is very difficult to get an appropriate and relevant answer without having some idea as to the question you are trying to resolve.

The following list of questions is meant to stimulate your thought process. Clearly, these are not all of the questions which should be asked, nor are all of them relevant to your particular firm at this particular time.

The more important point is that you modify your thinking to be certain to include the questioning process prior to the formulation of the plan statements.

PROBLEM QUESTIONS

1. What problems can be anticipated immediately? In the short term? In the long term?

Table 5-4

MANAGERIAL/PLAN STATEMENT MATRIX

	President	Admin. Asst.	VP Mfg.	Plant Mgr.	Purchasing & Distrib.	Mfg. Services	Production Mgr.	Maintenance Mgr.	Industrial Relations Mgr.	Engineering Mgr.
Office		1			6					
Sales	5	3			4					
New product design	5	3	2							
Labor force					8		5	2		2
Wage admin.		5			2		3	7	1	
Job evaluation					3	7	3		4	1
Personnel records		2					7		7	
Methods		5		7	8	7	7			1
Sample development	7	7	2	8						
Maintenance				4		7	4			
Plant safety				7			5	8		
Plant protection		4		4			7			
Production scheduling		3	8	4	4	7	2			
Delivery timetable	5	7		8	4		8	7		
Routing priorities		8				1	3			
Pricing	1	4								
Maintenance of production scheduling		4			3	8	8	4	1	
Expedite production orders	1	4			7	8	7	2		
Plant & purch.		3		4	1		4			
Quality control	5	3			7	8	8			2
Operations analysis		2					7			1
Control data		5					7			
Materials handling		4			7	2	8			
Layout of workplace		8				7	7			1

Code: 1 = does the work; 2 = Directly supervises; 3 = Consults with; 4 = Must notify; 5 = Administers general supervision; 6 = Coordinates and supervises; 7 = Discusses specifically submitted points; 8 = Participates in discussions.

2. What obstacles are preventing the company from reducing costs and becoming more efficient?

3. What changes can be made to enlarge responsibilities and currency in job requirements?

4. What policies, positions, organizational conditions or directives are holding back performance or growth improvements?

5. What is the length of the product's life span and how soon will it be potentially obsolescent?

OPPORTUNITY QUESTIONS

1. In what areas do the company's products have unique advantages over competing products? How can these areas be expanded?
2. Where does the company have product or service values that are most closely aligned with apparent customer needs?
3. In what areas does the company have the highest probable growth rate for its products or its services?
4. Where does the company have the greatest potential for technological breakthroughs? If this potential is pursued, what will the effects be on present facilities and equipment?
5. Where does the company have its greatest number of potential customers for volume sales with its emerging new technology?

PERSONNEL QUESTIONS

1. Who are the marginal or submarginal managers and employees who drain rather than enhance the organization's resources?
2. Which individuals would greatly improve their performance if they were aligned with new challenges or opportunities?
3. Which employees are impeding organizational improvements? What can be done to unblock this situation or to help people to bolster their performance?
4. Who are the employees who have worthwhile ideas but who are not able to implement them?
5. Who are the people who are too small for their big jobs and who are the people who are too big for their small jobs?

SCHEDULING QUESTIONS

1. When can the organization schedule changes which will reduce defects and rejects?
2. When can new cost projections be completed to meet new commitments?

3. When can additional personnel be added to meet prior commitments?

4. When can present commitments be moved up for a newer and a sooner completion date?

5. When can new scheduling be put into effect to get a new idea implemented?

METHODS QUESTIONS

1. Can our layout be revised to improve coordination of effort and to shorten distance?

2. How can the sequence of work assignments be changed or regrouped to reduce costs and to improve scheduling?

3. What rearrangement would improve satisfaction, morale and, especially, results?

4. What suboperation can be modified or even eliminated to improve the overall good of a major operation?

SUMMARY OF EFFECTIVE
PLAN FORMULATION PRINCIPLES

1. Recognize goal-seeking as the most important activity of leadership.

2. Set aside specific times for planning activities.

3. Establish specific, measurable goals in all areas of activity.

4. Involve others in a creative manner. The most creative way to involve aspiring professional managers is to appeal to their greed. A well-constructed incentive compensation plan based on performance measures-to-objectives offers a piece of the action to those managers who truly perform.

5. Provide the opportunity for training at all levels of supervision in planning.

6. Bring in an outside consultant who understands goal-seeking and who can act as a catalyst.

7. Create reminder cards and signs. Post these in prominent places; use the communications systems.

8. Establish control feedback and a system for continuous evaluation of plans and objectives.

9. Place the emphasis on goals rather than on methods to achieve them.

10. Always consider cost effectiveness.

11. See that short-range goals are coordinated with long-range goals.

6

PLAN
OBJECTIVES

The most important ingredient of successful plan implementation is recognition of the necessity to express plan objectives in quantitative, measurable and objective terms. If this is the first time that your firm is going through the planning and managerial performance process, you will find such measures are indispensable. In this process, we are finally translating the strategy statements made by the owners into discrete and quantifiable plan objectives for the firm.

In the following chapters, we will carry forward the plan objectives and translate them into managerial performance objectives. In turn, these objectives will lend themselves to audit and control of managerial performance as well as provide objective, impersonal measurements of incentive compensation rewards.

How does one begin to quantify and formulate plan objectives? Once again, we will follow the pattern established earlier of providing an intellectual context within which we can be assured of valid and relevant objective definitions:

• Objectives should be formulated in terms of what is to be accomplished, rather than what is to be avoided. Objectives, thus, are always developed in positive terms.

• Objectives should have specific deadlines for each achievement, so as to provide measurements and time references for actions.

• Objectives should be tied to an accountability statement which identifies a specific manager who is responsible for the accomplishment of the objective.

• Objectives should be written in concise and crisp statements. They should avoid irrelevant information, excessive descriptions or elaborate background detail.

• Objectives should be formulated to achieve a single, specific result. They should not be designed to broadly cover a multitude of involvements.

• Objectives should focus on what is to be achieved rather than upon the activities to be performed.

• Objectives should be stated forcefully, using action terms such as "complete by," "achieve," "replace" or "gain." Each statement should imply performance or results within a time frame.

• Objectives should be formulated so that they may be reviewed continuously, as projects develop, to determine what progress—or lack of it—is being made. A key factor here is to be able to analyze what is happening in terms of what has been planned, and to do so on an ongoing basis.

• Objectives should be developed after reviewing the applicable previous history of a project. A plan formulator who does not know past history is, to paraphrase a saying, doomed to repeat it.

• Objectives should be developed to reflect organizational needs, such as ROI, profits, schedules and personnel.

• Objectives should be fully communicated to the people involved, not only initially but whenever they are changed or updated. Results, also, should be posted openly and regularly.

• Objectives should be coordinated with the facilities, resources and skills within the organization.

• Objectives should have full documentation to provide the basis for performance measurement as the project develops and for future planning.

• Objectives should be assigned a numerical index or other measurement to indicate the anticipated probability of achievement.

• Objectives should be designed to fit the management team and the resources to be used.

• Objectives should be prioritized to give not only a ranking but a designated urgency.

• Objectives should be developed in such a manner that they are of significance to each individual as he or she carries out the responsibilities of the mission.

• Objectives should be formulated and developed so that they are a commitment between management and subordinates and all parts of the corporate team.

• Objectives should clearly express the key opportunities which give meaning to the effort and which make coordinated effort understandable and meaningful.

• And lastly, objectives should be written in quantifiable statements that can be easily measurable by anyone involved and just as easily reported.

Paying attention to these signposts, we are ready to move on to the quantification of objectives. There are some objectives which are "gimme's" in the sense that they are always applicable, always relevant, but alarmingly often overlooked. Some notable examples:

• Boost profits
• Achieve better share of the market
• Improve corporate effectiveness
• Streamline interdepartmental coordination
• Improve sales volume
• Work to get greatest efficiency
• Maintain highest possible quality
• Deliver better customer service
• Target in on cost effectiveness
• Coordinate for more timely assistance
• Communicate better with other departments
• Improve delivery times
• Continue present management procedures
• Lower costs of production
• Streamline existing procedures
• Improve plant working conditions
• Thorough study of new programs
• Gain industry-wide technical leadership
• Complete plan for future extingencies, quantified fifteen years out
• Totally decrease delay times
• Always maintain good labor relations

Speaking, then, to the need for *quantification*, it cannot be overstressed that the accounting system, while a valuable source of measurement data, is not and should not be the only source used to define plan objectives (or, for that matter, should it be the only source to measure managerial performance, as we shall see later). A common trap that the neophyte manager stumbles into is overreliance on the accounting system for objective data.

It must be recalled that the purpose of the accounting system is diametrically opposed to the purpose of planning. The accounting system can only look backward. It is concerned with history. It is retrospective.

The planning process, by contrast, is concerned only with the future. It is prospective.

Therefore, the role of the accounting system, at best, can merely be as a contributor to the monitoring and control aspects of the managerial performance measurement process.

Plan objectives can be, and, of course, should be expressed in terms other than dollars. The following list is meant to suggest other-than-dollar measurements for use in establishing plan objectives:

- Production units
- Time spans
- Volume measurements
- Averages
- Frequency ratios
- Indexes
- Proportions or percentages
- Ratios
- Aggregate of numbers
- Phases
- Degrees
- Cube utilization
- Percentiles
- Deciles
- Quartiles
- Mean deviations
- Correlations

Once again, the list presented is not intended to be exhaustive and complete; it is meant only to be suggestive. Of course, be mindful that you bear the task of preparing and using a list tailored to your particular firm at your particular time. Despite that qualifier, it's really not a bad place to start.

In addition to that list of non–accounting data system measures, how should these measurements be related? In other words, while we may have data from the real world rather than the dusty ledgers, how should we translate them and marry them to plan objectives?

The following list presents some suggested uses of objectives for planning purposes. The discerning reader will note that the following lists are usable in the context of managerial performance measures as well as plan-level objectives.

In other words, we are borderline between personal accountability objectives and company-wide plan objectives. This is a very healthy place to be; because it suggests that if we have done a sufficiently careful job of strategy and plan definitions then we can build upon this foundation to reach individuals within the firm who are responsible and accountable for specific performance.

- Employee absenteeism and turnover rates
- Failures to meet sales quotas by salesperson, by territory or by outlet

- Numbers of customer payments not received
- Numbers of employee grievances
- Numbers of accidents
- Budget variances exceeding target levels
- Maximum, minimum or low-limit of inventories
- Employee hours worked exceeding target levels
- Ratio or percentage of rejects in items received
- Percentages of shortages of scheduled material for production
- Significant percentage variances between requisitions per month and that which was forecast
- Change between supplier deliveries and contracted for quality
- Change in the average total costs of handling a requisition
- Change in time required between a decision to purchase and actual time of purchase order issuance
- Inventory reports of items below minimum point
- Cost analysis of inventory items with dollar amounts in excess of pre-determined percentage of total inventory
- Status reports of orders held by the accounting department which are more than seventy-two hours old
- Accounts receivable trial balances pinpointing only balances over a predetermined number of days
- Actual product sales, as opposed to budgeted sales, for any line over or under budget by a certain percentage

Now, then: Please go back and *reread* the preceding list of measurements and extract from it the principle that you may have missed, which is *management by exception*.

Do not fail—*repeat do not fail*—in establishing plan objectives to provide *for, and to build in, management-by-exception reporting.*

Objectives are expressed as a number, but performances very rarely—except by coincidence—match that particular number. In other words, performance will always be above or below an objective level. That's not important. What is important is the magnitude of the variances as well as the trend of the variance.

As an effective manager, you are well aware that time is your most important adversary, as discussed in *No Nonsense Management*. Therefore, you maximize use of your time and your organization's time by focusing only on those items which show significant (however that is defined for each particular objective) variance of performance from objective.

Earlier, I provided you with a list of "gimme's." But again, there are a number of additional factors that may or may not be important in your firm during this particular planning cycle. They are not really "gimme's" but they are important from the standpoint of being given ample consideration.

Approach this list with the question: "Because we observe these symptoms, should we establish planning objectives for any of the following items?"

- Low profitability
- High number of shipping returns
- Ineffective or nonproductive advertising
- Loss of important customers
- Production delays
- Excessive backlogs
- Higher-than-anticipated costs
- Slow or no sales growth
- Large overhead expenses
- Slippage of schedules
- High rates of spoilage or waste
- High repair rates
- Excessive machine downtime
- Rising costs of material handling
- Unacceptable rejection rates
- Decline or change in sales volume
- High overtime trends
- Repeated errors
- Interdepartmental disputes or disruptive rivalries
- Individual or departmental resistance to change
- Quantities of corrective work
- Unplanned low inventories
- Excessive personnel turnover
- Uneven quality control
- Lack of sufficient dividends
- High rates of absenteeism
- Increasing pilferage
- Quantity of grievances
- Widespread low morale
- Overactive rumor mill
- Poor public relations

The previously expressed caveat also painfully applies here: The list is not meant to be all-inclusive. Instead, it is provided to stimulate your thinking as well as that of your organization.

From the general manager's standpoint, or from the chief executive officer's standpoint, there are seven plan objectives which must, *repeat must*, be included for definition, monitoring and control follow-up reporting:

1. Profits as percent of capital employed (ROI)
2. Profits as percent of sales (ROS)
3. Sales as a multiple of capital employed
4. Sales as a multiple of fixed assets
5. Sales as a multiple of inventory
6. Sales per employee
7. Profits per employee

Rather than discuss the plan objectives on a functional level basis, the following list speaks only to the plan objectives related to the shareholder's primary interest in your firm—profit. The functional treatment of objectives will be explored in detail in subsequent chapters. But in this chapter, saving the dessert for last, the following list of objectives encompasses profit impact. *It is to these objectives that, of course, primary attention should be given.* We will see later how this key list of objectives will be translated into and supported by functional managerial objectives.

PERFORMANCE INDICATORS

- Percentage of increase in dividends
- Rate of sales growth and profile of the sales growth
- ROI percentage
- Ratio of profits to assets
- Upturn in net operating income
- Debt ratios to total assets
- Ratio of sales per employee
- Debt to equity fund ratio
- Rate of customer complaints and accompanying inputs
- Percentage of net profit to sales
- Overhead costs and drift ratios
- Trends in sales cost proportions and related data
- Deviations from standard costs
- Size and frequency of sales orders
- Transportation costs as a percentage of sales levels and orders
- Sales orders and levels variable cost rates
- Market share (actual and potential percentages)
- Ratio of current liabilities to current assets
- Trends and collectibility ratios of accounts receivable
- Employee recruitment costs
- Labor (direct and indirect) ratios
- Marginal cost trends and ratios

7

HOW TO SET
MANAGEMENT PERFORMANCE
STANDARDS

You possess a great deal of perserverance and commitment in your pursuit of managerial excellence to have reached this point in the book. If you have understood all that has come before, you are well on your way to becoming an excellent manager.

This chapter is the pivotal chapter in the book and clearly the most critical. Thus far we have extracted (and extracted is really an appropriate word) from the owners of the business their definitive statements of how they want their investment managed.

We have taken a long-term look at where we want to go with the firm, and we have defined some relatively short-term goals and objectives which will lead us toward and along the paths of strategy earlier defined.

What we are about to do is translate all of this "good stuff" into personal measurements for individual managers. In the succeeding chapters, you will obtain thorough and complete beginning "checklists" upon which to build individual objective measurement programs.

But the purpose of this chapter is really to provide you with an overview of performance standards so that you may approach them in a manner which supports, and even helps to achieve, the strategies and plans of the owners and, at the same time, fulfill your primary management obligations to your subordinates. The latter task is concerned with providing an environment of opportunity for individual and personal professional growth and development.

The proper perspective for understanding performance standards requires that we begin by looking at the performance standards for the firm. Remember that personal performance standards for managers, while they may be very precise and very well qualified, are totally irrelevant and counter-productive if they fail to corroborate, support and fulfill the performance standards of the firm. Figure 7-1 illustrates, in a rather simplistic overview, the ultimate performance standards of any for-profit organization.

The earning power of a firm is the ultimate measure by which further investment, by either the debt or the equity route, will be either encouraged or discouraged. So as you proceed through succeeding chapters in finalizing the objectives for your functional managers, do not forget for a moment that the bullseye is really the enhancement of the earning power of your firm.

In order to understand and to gain some insight into these various performance standards by which your firm will be measured both in the marketplace and in the financial community, look at the following list of thirteen component elements. When these elements are taken together, they largely determine the value of your firm's earning power.

1. Current Ratio:

$$\frac{\text{Current Assets}}{\text{Current Liabilities}}$$

Net working capital is arrived at by dividing the firm's current assets by its current liabilities. An unusually low current ratio indicates that a company may face difficulty in meeting its bills. On the other hand, an unusually high current ratio suggests that a firm is not applying sufficient funds to corporate growth objectives.

2. Percentage Composition of Current Assets
3. Acid Test or Quick Ratio:

$$\frac{\text{Cash} + \text{A/C Receivable} + \text{Marketable Securities}}{\text{Current Liabilities}}$$

4. Receivables Turnover:

$$\frac{\text{Annual Credit Sales}}{\text{Average Trade A/C Receivable}}$$

This mathematical model measures the liquidity of a firm's receivables. For example, if the annual rate of turnover is six times, this indicates that the average receivable will be collected in two months. An unusually high turnover of accounts receivable for any particular line of business may indicate an unnecessarily tight credit policy that is limiting sales volume by driving away slower paying customers. In contrast, an unusually low turnover of accounts receivable would indicate a congestion of funds that reduce the available flow of funds for reinvestment in growth. But if a

FIGURE 7-1
Ultimate Performance Standards

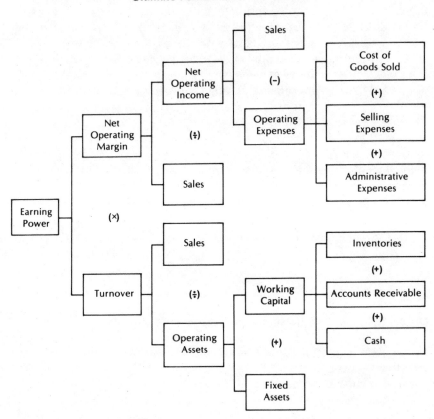

company is experiencing a sharp growth in sales, or when its sales are primarily seasonal, care must be taken in applying the receivables turnover test.

5. Inventory Turnover:

$$\frac{\text{Cost of Goods Sold}}{\text{Average Inventory}}$$

The inventory turnover figure provides data on whether the inventory is excessive or deficient in relation to a firm's volume of sales. An unusually high turnover in inventory, contrary to popular wisdom, is not especially beneficial. In a manufacturing firm, for example, efforts to continue an especially high turnover of raw material may be penalized by running out of items so that production lines are shut down, resulting in pre-tax impact certainly, and loss of volume probably.

6. Debt to Net Worth:

$$\frac{\text{Total Debt}}{\text{Tangible Net Worth}}$$

The Debt to Net Worth ratio shows the dollars the creditors lent in relation to the dollars the owners have invested. The corporation's Net Worth is defined as the sum of any outstanding preferred stock, common stock, surplus, undivided profits and any surplus reserve (such as "reserve for contingencies)." Intangible assets are deducted from net worth determination since these assets are usually difficult to measure in terms of their actual value or earning power. Secondly, some intangible assets, such as "goodwill," are often of value to the company only if it continues as a growing concern. In general, use debt for "plan" time intervals and equity for "strategy" time intervals.

7. Times—Interest—Earned:

$$\frac{\text{Preinterest, Pretax Earnings}}{\text{Annual Interest Charges}}$$

8. Times—Dividends—Earned:

$$\frac{\text{After Tax Earnings}}{\text{Dividend Requirement}}$$

9. Earnings Per Share
10. Price/Earnings Ratio
11. Payout Ratio:

$$\frac{\text{Dividends/Share}}{\text{Earnings/Share}}$$

12. Return on Residual Earnings

$$\frac{\text{Earnings (after taxes, minus preferred dividends)}}{\text{Common Stock + Surplus}}$$

The earnings available to the common stockholders divided by the number of shares outstanding yields a figure for earnings per share. This figure may then be compared to the price per share quoted in the market to derive a price–earnings ratio. If the quoted market price were $48, and the annual earnings per share were $4, then the price-earnings would be 12 to 1.

13. Operating Ratio:

$$\frac{\text{Total Operating Expense + Cost of Goods Sold}}{\text{Net Sales}}$$

A 100 percent operating ratio is equal to the net operating margin. Net sales minus the cost of goods sold equals the gross margin.

Now, then: shifting focus from the firm to management, it might not be a bad idea to consider what are the various functions and the duties which any "manager" must fulfill.

At the risk of overgeneralization, but in the attempt to provide you with an overview, the following list provides a "handy dandy" overall view of what a manager does:

• Sets goals and performance criteria.

• Provides incentives so that subordinates want to reach goals and meet performance criteria.

• Gives regular objective "feedback" so that people know where they stand in their work.

• Organizes the overall work process, plans for its execution and establishes priorities.

• Uses techniques of "participative management" whereby employees participate when it is appropriate in decisions which affect them and their work.

• Personally orients important new employees and sees that appropriate subordinates teach him or her the job to be done the way the company wants it done. Does not rely on the "world's worst trainer" to orient or to train a new employee—the person who is just leaving a job.

• Holds regular, two-way communicative meetings with subordinates.

• Is careful of the use of his or her rank in the company and demonstrates this through courtesy to peers and subordinates, respect for the ideas of others, and through his or her tact, understanding of the needs of others.

• Creates a good "model" for others to follow, including dressing suitably for one's position or for the occasion. Is punctual and seldom late for work, maintains mental and physical health, and shows genuine positive thinking toward his or her work and the company in general.

• Is flexible, willing to try new methods and procedures, is tolerant of new people and influences within the organization, and is willing to accept constant—and accelerating—change.

• Has mastered a systematic method of problem solving which is both consistent in its approach and known by all subordinates. He or she considers all alternatives before making a decision, and having once made it, sticks with it. Establishes procedures to aid in future routine decision-making so all can understand and use them.

• Takes pride in managing a cohesive and positive work force, whose energies and enthusiasms are linked with known goals and objectives. He or she takes pride in having a good "team" in place, with everyone knowing the right signals, and the team in turn having confidence in top management.

• Encourages a certain amount of "flex" in the operation to meet new circumstances and challenges. Does not go by the book so pendantically that he or she cannot manage by exception, when needed.

• Has a statesmanlike stance in viewing new challenges and problems, and can positively view new inputs from the standpoint of the total organization's needs, rather than from just the restrictive viewpoint of his or her own specialty or department.

• Is a good team player. He or she observes the organization's rules, written and unwritten, on most occasions. Follows the direction of higher level executives with consideration and care most of the time. He or she also takes care to know the full capabilities of the team under him or her, as well as its limitations. Takes time to develop subordinates' capabilities through personal instruction, and, especially, systematic training.

• Is a hard worker, and such work as he or she performs is of high quality and absolutely understood, easily measured through observable performances, and fairly applied. Both "boss" and "employee" should be linked together toward specific accomplishments through a performance system.

Now, being mindful that we are structuring our performance standards so that they are consistent with, and supportive of, the performance standards of the firm, and having grasped a general overview of how the manager/ human being works, let's proceed to discuss the use to which performance standards should be tailored.

The establishment of performance standards and the publication of them will be an exercise in futility unless they can be reported upon regularly, consistently, quantitatively and with relative accuracy. So it is of great use to us in the establishment of these performance standards to *have the end use in mind.* What are some of these end use targets that we need to pay attention to? Let's look at these, one at a time:

CONTROL ENHANCEMENT FACTORS	PERFORMANCE ENHANCEMENT POTENTIAL
1. Timeliness	To be useful, information must be provided on a timely and current basis to meet present and anticipated needs.
2. Reliability	Data are properly checked out, reported with accuracy so that by themselves they can be factored as inputs to a managerial decision.

3. Efficiency

Data for performance enhancement are routinely generated in quantity through an efficient system. A rule of thumb here is that the data be pertinent to the needs of management and the system not be so efficient that it produces more than is needed. The cost of gathering, evaluating and processing the data should not outweigh their value.

4. Responsibility

Data are provided with accountability and responsibility as to both timing and generation. The information provided should be related to the actual needs of the persons involved and at a level consistent with their responsibilities and span of control.

5. Exception

Data generated are on situations which go beyond norms and which need to be brought to management's attention. Information thus "pinpoints" exceptions or potential trouble spots.

6. Compliance

Data are provided to meet preset reporting needs of the organization.

7. Comparative

Provides ratios, comparisons between sets of data for evaluative purposes. For example: budget year-to-date. Or actual sales compared with projected sales.

8. Unified data base

The data base is coordinated for more effective information processing and understanding. For example, actual expenditures vs. budget can be correlated for an at-a-glance readout.

9. Performance measures incorporated into data base

Provides statistical data on quantified performance standards. Eliminates guesswork and "the human element" through the use of the same rigors and controls as used for financial data. Provides "objective" viewpoints and greatly increases accuracy.

10. Planning/forecast system

Sets up the process for preparation of plans and forecasts, with projections and possible pinpointing of trends.

11. Automated budget compilation

Quickly generates budget data, allows breakouts of budget data for study, aids in presenting budget data for reports.

12. Automated currency conversion

Improves financial reporting timeliness by automatically converting foreign currency amounts into the applicable nation's currency. Also, allows multiple-nation currency reporting within one system.

13. Multiple company processing

Lets an independent company or division control its own inputs separately, when used within a company-wide financial data base.

14. Flexible report format

Changing informational needs can be accommodated without costly programming changes for the computer.

15. Account transaction data analysis

Retrieves and analyzes account transaction data in addition to data on an account's balance.

16. On-line processing

Allows instantaneous updating and editing of data at the time they are entered into the system.

| 17. Data base | Breaks out the data base |
| management system | from the application programming. |

At the risk of some redundancy, *one of the essential inputs that must be obtained is the knowledge of how performance standards for management should be structured.* For example, what should they look like? And what are some of the principles that should be borne in mind as we define standards?

The following list of *twelve structural requirements* is presented for your review and selection. This is one set of pages that I would "dog ear" so that the information is readily available to you as you go through the performance standard setting process.

TWELVE GOAL STRUCTURAL REQUIREMENTS

1. Goals will define final results that are to be achieved.
2. Goals will be specific and measurable.
3. Goals will always be in writing and communicated to all who need to know.
4. Goals will represent work essential to meet higher-level goals.
5. Individual goals will support functional goals, and these, in turn, will support the organization's needs.
6. When there are several goals, each goal must be prioritized in advance.
7. Concurrence on the goals to be achieved will be reached by those affected by the goals or those who do the work described by the goals.
8. Balance must be kept between short-term and long-term goals, consistent with perceived needs of the firm.
9. Final goals can only be developed after individual items are negotiated between groups and management. The negotiated items may include standards, resources and schedules.
10. Individual goals will not conflict or overlap with those assigned to other individuals (but there must not be any "gaps" in the work to be accomplished).
11. If all of the individual goals are met, then the goals of the division or the group will also be met.
12. Each manager will personally participate in the goal setting process to be certain that each goal is both challenging and consistent with overall planning.

Until this point, we have focused on where the firm is going, where the owners want it to go, and how we can establish objectives and milestones at both the strategic and plan level for getting there.

However, when constructing performance standards for managers, your time-frame is necessarily very short and traditionally embraces only the fiscal accounting year.

Before you proceed to try to take the firm where the owners want it to go, it is most prudent to *gain an in-depth understanding of where you currently are*. The following questions, when thoroughly and honestly answered, will provide you with an unprecedentedly clear and lucid *snapshot of your present position*. The answers to these questions will enable you to gauge the degree of difficulty and the areas of difficulty which you can anticipate, even as you permeate the managerial race with personal accountability.

PERFORMANCE TESTS FOR MANAGEMENT

1. Does your management team spend a lot of its time "fire-fighting" problems rather than preventing them in the first place?

2. Do your top managers properly delegate authority with responsibility so that they refrain from making decisions that their subordinates should be making?

3. Are your managers primarily guided by market or customer needs rather than theoretical concepts or proprietary interests?

4. Is there a strong sense of urgency coupled with an understanding of responsibility among your managers? Or is there a general "pass-the-buck" attitude?

5. Do all your managers know what to do as well as how to do it? And do they act accordingly?

6. Do your managers and their subordinates have a clear insight into their work priorities so they may spend the major portion of their activities on those work areas of greatest importance to the organization?

7. Is there an open atmosphere in which management members may freely share views and mutually determine solutions to common problems? Or is there a power struggle, with clearly defined adversary relationships, which makes some groups operate in "secret" and withhold information?

8. Is there an even balance between authority and individual self-discipline so that both individual initiative and teamwork can be operative?

9. Is there a line of succession in depth for management so that the organization knows who will replace whom and that these "successors" have proper training?

10. Do managers hold regularly scheduled conferences, with agendas, as well as impromptu meetings to solve mutual problems? Do they communicate well between meetings?

11. Is there an atmosphere of "trust" within the organization so that a certain number of "mistakes" can be risked? Are past mistakes explained openly and used positively as a learning experience so that managers learn from them?

12. Is the organization a vibrant one, creating new ideas and solutions—or is "don't-rock-the-boat" conformity the operative phrase?

13. Does your management team have successors in place and ready to go should any sudden vacancy occur?

14. Has your company ever had a systematic analysis of its performance? Or a study of its performance in terms of product or product design?

15. Are company objectives and goals defined and written in clear statements so that everyone knows exactly where the company is headed and what its immediate plans are? Have these statements been printed and distributed to all employees?

16. Are the written goals and objectives understood, favored and accepted by all key personnel?

17. Has an allocation of time, energy, money and resources been made to achieve corporate goals and objectives? Or are these largely "theoretical?"

18. Are clear objectives spelled out to each department to contribute to the overall objectives of the organization?

19. Are recurring questions identified, and are standardized procedures set up for dealing with them?

20. Are decisions within your company made after carefully and quantitatively considering alternatives and risks?

21. Does your company provide every manager with standard policy and procedures guidelines in written form which will cover most of the recurring important decisions he or she will have to make?

22. Are your company's systems and procedures documented and distributed to those who need to know and use them?

23. Does your company have someone formally in charge of maintaining, updating, producing and distributing all formal documents pertaining to systems and procedures?

24. Does your company have all general policies, rules, regulations and other pertinent information compiled in an easy-to-use manual or guidebook?

25. Have standards been established for such a manual's format, content or scope?

26. Does the company have controls to make certain that all information is kept current and in the hands of the people who will use it? Are the materials dated for reference and review? Systematically changed?

27. Does your company provide financial statements to all managers who should have them to do their job? Is the information understandable? Have all managers had sufficient training to analyze and understand the statements?

28. Are your company's budgets prepared with the inputs of the managers who will be responsible for meeting them? Are budgets carefully constructed and approved on the basis of planned estimates from all pertinent and applicable sources (or guessed at by an extrapolation from previous performance)?

29. Are the final budgets realistic, timely and attainable?

30. Does your company plan for a specific ROI? Does it track its ROI at regular scheduled intervals?

31. If your company's ROI computation appears inadequate, does your company have specific plans to improve it?

32. What is your company's return on gross assets? If not up to par, does the company have an operable strategy to change the bottom line?

33. Are company problems evaluated so that profitability will not be adversely affected? Are problems which bear on profitability given a top priority?

34. Has your company a fixed ratio of managers and personnel to costs? From industry standards is this "fat" or is it excessively "lean?"

35. Does your company have in effect a systematic and objective compensation plan with clearly stated standards of performance as the basis for salary increases?

36. Do all the company's employees understand the performance standards?

37. Is management itself accountable for performance standards, which are objective and measurable by all?

38. Is the basic operating philosophy of your company one which treats its human resources as basically intelligent, understanding and capable?

39. Does your management team maintain a minumum of centralized control in needed areas while at the same time delegating large amounts of power and authority to the lowest operative level?

40. Does your company try to develop its managerial team by new assignments and changing responsibilities as well as through specialized and pertinent training?

41. Are the present and potential managerial forces in your company picked solely on the basis of past track record as well as proven ability? Are performers promoted quickly?

42. Does your company add new services as soon as they become known while routinely modifying or phasing out older services? Has this been done in the last six months? Last two years? Or not at all in the past five years? Is there a general stagnation in improving services?

43. Does your company enjoy good relations in the community it is a part of? Do surveys or audits show generally positive feelings toward it on the part of employees? Suppliers? Neighbors? Professional affiliates? Or even competitors?

44. Does your company have a favorable relationship with stock-holders and investors? Or is there open hostility between these and management, with eruptions likely at annual meetings?

Now that you have gained a profound knowledge of the current state of your organization and you more perfectly understand the principles and the structural goals of performance standards studied, you are ready to launch.

But a launch, at least in this day and age, cannot really be performed without a countdown. So the following list is presented to provide insight for you to govern the launch into a very adventuresome part of management.

I caution the reader that the list is *not* presented incorrectly.

The list really is numbered from six down to one to stimulate your going into managerial orbit through the remaining chapters of this book.

Six-Step Countdown

6. Create a working climate in which your managers can increase motivation for individuals and team contribution through focusing on results rather than activities.

5. Develop logical parameters within which your managers can direct, control and assist in the overall objectives to be accomplished. Reward results.

4. Systematize procedures, standardize performance levels and communicate both to your managers. Use ample communications techniques, such as conferences and meetings, to identify needs and keep everyone posted.

3. Link overall goals with individual jobs so that everyone's work fits into the overall objectives.

2. Coach individual team members in performance needs and ways to achieve individual objectives.

1. Make certain everyone has a full sense of identity in overall objectives and feels he or she has a significant job in reaching the sought-for performance levels.

8

HOW TO MEASURE MARKETING MANAGEMENT PERFORMANCE

Probably one of the best sources of individual objective measurements in a marketing function is the market plan itself.

For those rare, few readers who are unfamiliar with a market plan, the following market plan outline is presented. Here you will see quickly that many of the subheadings begin to identify quantified and measurable individual performance objectives.

It is urged that you give more than casual perusal to the subheadings in this market plan outline, because you will see later in this chapter considerable overlap of the lists of suggested objectives with the contents of a well-prepared marketing plan.

MARKETING PLAN OUTLINE

A. WHAT DO WE HAVE TO SELL? FOR HOW LONG?
   Name of product
   Function
   Use
   Expected life cycle
   Special features
   Etc.

B. TO WHOM WILL WE SELL IT?
    Composition
    Size
    Geographic location
    Characteristics
    Requirements
    Names of specific people, if possible

C. WHAT IS OUR COMPETITION?
    Names
    Feature and use comparison
    Price comparison
    Delivery comparison

D. WHAT ARE WE TRYING TO ACCOMPLISH?
    State of objectives
    Product sales in
        Units
        Dollars
        Market share
        By varying time period

E. WHAT TECHNIQUES WILL WE USE?
    Costs (by increments)
    Pricing philosophy
    Distribution plan by geographical area
    Marketing theme and basic product appeal to customer
    Delivery schedules
    Payment terms
    Guarantees and warranty
    Tie-in sales

F. HOW WILL WE INTRODUCE THE PRODUCT?
    Launch program:
        in-house sales force
        distributors
        product announcement
    Sales call plan

G. HOW DO WE MOTIVATE THE SALES FORCE?
    Incentive programs:
        regional and individual quotas
        commissions

contests
special promotions, etc.
Reporting

H. WHAT WILL THIS DO TO OUR OTHER PRODUCTS?
Volumes
Units
Redesign of other products in line to match new one
Inventory reduction of old stock

I. WHY, WHAT, WHEN AND HOW ARE WE GOING TO ADVERTISE?
Objectives
Budget
Major and minor themes
Ad schedules
Strategy and schedule for relating ad program to field sales effort
Follow-up plans

J. CAN WE "RIFLE" AS WELL AS "SHOTGUN" THE MARKET?
Objectives
Budget
Mailing list
Strategy and schedule for relating direct mail program to field sales effort

K. HOW TO PLAY "HOST" WITH MAXIMUM RETURN?
Objectives
Budget
Schedule of events and dates
Themes
Strategy and schedules for utilizing participation for maximum field sales
    effort
Follow-up plans

L. HOW CAN WE GET ADDITIONAL EXPOSURE?
Objectives
Budget
Themes
Techniques:
    outside agency
    press releases
    technical papers
    etc.

M. HOW DO WE TRAIN OUR OWN PEOPLE TO SELL THE PRODUCTS?
Objectives
Budget
Techniques
Schedule
Props and publications needed—and schedule for obtaining

N. HOW DO WE TEACH THE CUSTOMER THE USE AND BENEFITS OF THE PRODUCT?
Objectives
Budget
Techniques
Schedule
Props and publications needed—and schedule for obtaining

O. HOW ARE WE GOING TO ORGANIZE TO KEEP THE PRODUCT OPERATING IN WARRANTY?
Policy
Strategy for use as sales tool
Anticipated cost

P. WHAT ARE WE GOING TO DO AND HOW AFTER WARRANTY EXPIRES?
Policy
Strategy for use as sales tool
Budgeted cost or sales and profit

Q. HOW DO WE USE SPARE PARTS TO BUILD SALES AND PROFITS?
Distribution policy
Pricing policy
Strategy
Budgeted sales and profit

R. HOW WILL WE INFORM PROSPECT
Catalogs, spec sheets, tech. manuals, other publications, etc.
Quantity
Distribution
Schedule

S. HOW DO WE SUPPORT SALES EFFORT WITH PRODUCT?
Policy
Levels
Strategy

T. WHAT "PROPS" WILL THE SALES FORCE NEED—AND WHEN?
Models or samples
Films and audio-visual equipment
Drawings and blueprints
Pictures
Advertising portfolio
Visual sales presentation
Other new equipment
Testimonial letters
Documented profit and/or savings presentation
Etc.

After seven and a half chapters of preparation, we have finally arrived at a point where we can present suggested lists of individual performance objectives.

This is the same pattern that you will find in succeeding chapters through number 22. They may or may not, individually, be directly applicable to your company. They are meant and intended only to provide you with a "checklist" and as a source of ideas for objective measurements.

Obviously, the set of objectives chosen for your firm in all cases and for all functions must be carefully tailored so that they are relevant to your firm.

I wish I could do more for you, but that would require occupying your position, which I don't think you are prepared to relinquish.

Management Marketing/Background Data

1. What is the size of your total market?
2. What share of the market do you have?
3. What is your competitor's share of the market?
4. How effective is your marketing support (on a scale of 1 to 10):
    • Advertising?
    • Promotion?
    • Public Relations?
    • Technical Services?
5. What are the factors that determine your market size and nature?
    • regional
    • national
    • international
    • economic
    • governmental
    • other
6. What are your sales forecasts for your market
    • this year?

- next year?
- five years from now?

7. What are the main marketing methods you use?
   How effective are they?
   How effective are those of your competitors?
8. What are your distribution methods?
   How effective are they?
   How effective are they in comparison to those used by your competitors?
9. What are your main marketing advantages?
   Your competitors'?
10. How effective is your sales performance
    - for market or target penetration?
    - in comparison with forecast sales?
    - in comparison to sales expenses?
    - in comparison with customer complaint analysis?
    - in comparison with new accounts analysis?
    - for lost orders?
11. How effective is customer service
    - delivery?
    - scheduling?
    - customer satisfaction?
    - expenses?
    - activity?
12. What is your profitability:
    - by customer category?
    - by type of distributor?
    - by geographical area?
    - by product line?
13. What is the overall "health" of the dealer organization?
    What trends are apparent?

Examples of Specific Marketing Objectives

The XYZ company will:

14. Increase sales revenues of product X by N percent within N months by concentrating N promotion dollars in the Y marketing area.
15. Achieve N percent distribution in markets A, B, C and D of X marketing area.
16. Train all area representatives in training program T by N date to market Product X by N date.

17. Complete plans and statements by X date to introduce X new products by X date in Market Y.
18. Upgrade the ratio of sales per employee from X dollars to Y dollars by X date, and to Z dollars by N date.
19. Improve percentages of sales from X, Y and Z percentages within N market area to A, B and C, respectively, by N date.
20. Complete X percent of all follow-up calls for new inquiries within X days of receipt of calls.
21. Contract with N wholesalers by X date to handle N new merchandising by Y date according to marketing plan Z and prearranged schedule A.
22. Increase product turnover from T to X within N months.
23. Maintain sales expense to N percent of total sales while increasing sales force N percent during the fiscal year.
24. Initiate new system X to process orders while expediting the filling of back orders at the rate of N percent per day until N percent of back orders are filled. When N percent of back order levels are reached, then reinstate system Z.
25. Reduce by N percent the average handling time of all customer statements.
26. Increase X ratio by N percent from a monthly ratio of Y to Z percent while maintaining T pricing structure.
27. Reduce the number of complaints in W division from X to Y percent of invoices. Financial settlements applicable are not to exceed Z percent of billings of the division's total invoices per month.

Standards for Sales Promotion Responsibilities

28. Develop specific promotion ideas and detailed cost and work plans identifying the major tasks to be accomplished. This plan will be used as a managing and scheduling tool.
29. Complete public relations and trade relations projects including media contact for specific promotional opportunities. Write and secure placement for press releases and other publicity materials.
30. Develop direct mail campaigns to:
    • dealers
    • distributors
    • agents
    • consumers
31. Coordinate promotion tasks with advertising, sales and marketing operations.
32. Develop displays and materials for point of sale.
33. Develop, write and publish annual reports.

34. Produce sales aids including:
    - brochures or booklets
    - videotapes, films or slide shows
    - product literature
    - flip charts
    - giveaways, samples or other "demonstration" material
    - catalogs, reprints or price sheets
    - diagrams or models
35. Distribute promotional material to all applicable prospects and media contacts. Develop and maintain media, prospect and other mailing list and list sources.
36. Coordinate trade show or consumer exhibits.
37. Arrange for customer or prospect group hospitality.
38. Develop, write and publish external and internal house organs.
39. Plan and execute:
    - New branch openings
    - Plant openings, remodelings
    - Open houses
    - Special events
40. Coordinate promotional work with salespeople and with distributors.
41. Arrange clinics, seminars or educational presentations on the company's products or pertaining to the professional or technical knowledge involved in the company products, designs, developments, or standards.
42. Publish training manuals, training audio visual tapes, training slide shows or training videotapes.
43. Develop sales contests for salespeople, employees, distributors, agents, dealers or consumers.
44. Aid in the development of packaging.
45. Work with coupons, premiums and trial offers to boost sales.
46. Arrange cooperative advertising and promotional efforts or tie-ins.
47. Take charge of sales meetings, conventions and other meeting arrangements.
48. Assume responsibility for upgrading company correspondence, including:
    - Check through all departments for letters and redevelop as necessary.

    - Develop cover letters for mailings and advertising programs.
    - Draft "special occasion" letters.
    - Develop model letters for collection purposes
    - Develop sales letters for:
    introduction of a salesperson before the first call

follow-up after the first call

"thank you" for customer inquiry

maintaining communications between sales calls

thanking customer for the first order or repeat orders

49. Sell all promotion planning, budgets and materials to everyone concerned, from salespeople to corporate management.

Sales Performance Measurements for Marketing Management

50. Total sales of company
51. Projected company sales
52. Sales quotas
53. New account sales
54. Sales of new products
55. New products and new accounts sales
56. Calculated market potential for all sales predicted
57. Calls made by salespeople:
    - total number actually made
    - total made on new accounts only
58. Quotations made for potential sales:
    - total
    - new accounts
    - new products
    - new accounts and new products

59. Number of orders:
    - total
    - new accounts
    - new products
    - new accounts and new products

60. Number of accounts:
    - total
    - number sold in last fiscal year
    - new accounts opened and sold in fiscal year
    - top potential bracket only
    - potential of those in top potential bracket
61. Units sold (product)
62. Gross margin (products & total)
63. Expenses (with and without breakdown)
64. Direct costs
65. Contribution margin

Ration Analysis Data for Sales Management

66. Total sales divided by:
    - total quotations
    - total orders

- quota
- total expenses
- expense as percentage of sales
- salesperson per day
- total calls
- total potential
- top potential bracket
- potential of top potential bracket

67. Ratio of quotations:
    - total quotations divided by total calls
    - new account quotations divided by new account calls
    - new product quotations divided by new account calls
    - new product quotations divided by total calls
    - quoted new product sales divided by total quotations in dollars

68. New account sales divided by:
    - total sales
    - new account calls
    - new account quotes
    - new account orders

69. New products sales divided by:
    - total sales
    - total calls
    - new account calls
    - new product quotes
    - new product orders

70. Ratio of orders:
    - total orders divided by person divided by working days
    - total quoted orders divided by total quotations
    - total orders divided by total quotations
    - total orders divided by 100 calls
    - new account orders divided by new account quotations
    - new account orders divided by new account calls

71. Ratio of accounts sold:
    - number of accounts sold divided by total number of accounts
    - number of accounts in top potential bracket sold divided by total number in category

72. Sales expenses divided by total calls
73. Number of calls divided by person per day
74. Units sold divided by man per day
75. New accounts opened and sold in the last fiscal year and the trend shown

Sales Management Objectives by Product Line

76. Market potential to be achieved

77. Total sales volume to be gained
78. Sales as a percentage of potential market to be reached
79. Total marketing costs (quantitative):
    • call costs
    • service costs
    • delivery costs
    • marketing administration costs
    • marketing research costs
    • advertising and promotional costs
80. Marketing costs as a percentage of sales not to be exceed
81. Gross margin to be achieved
82. Profit contribution to be earned (volume less value added costs)
83. Profit contribution rate (percent of volume)
84. Product net profit to be achieved
85. Gross margin as a percentage of total sales
86. Profit contribution as a percent of total sales
87. Profit as a percentage of total sales
88. Total number of customers to be sold
89. Volume to be sold divided by the number of customers sold
90. Total calls and service and delivery costs divided by the number of customers
91. Net profit divided by sales
92. Inventory to be maintained
93. Cost of goods sold in relationship to inventory
94. Total investment
95. Net profit divided by sales
96. Sales divided by investment
97. Return on investment to be achieved
98. Break even point to be reached
99. Factor for safety to be maintained (volume minus break-even point) divided by break even point.

Marketing Management Standards for Monitoring Performance

100. Achievement of both short- and long-range negotiated goals for profit and for return on investment.
101. Achievement of subgoals for regions, districts and territories for volume, share and profit contribution rate.
102. Achievement of sales performance goals for calls per day, calls per person, expenses per call, order per call and volume per order.
103. Obtain a volume-mix goal by N date
104. Achieve advertising objectives set for coverage, readership, sales and costs.

105. Increase the profit contribution per salesperson by N percent within N months
106. Increase Product A's volume by N percent in each of the next N years by developing a new use or appeal for the product.
107. Keep marketing research costs within specified parameters of N costs per dollar of sales
108. Achieve product goals set for total, regions and districts on volume, share and profit
109. Achieve occupancy and volume goals for specified new products by N date
110. Achieve product return on investment goals for total, regions and districts
111. Achieve a maximum N month moving average R & D cost per dollar of new product profit

Marketing Management Measurement Ratios

112. Sales this year divided by base year sales
113. Sales growth in real (adjusted) terms
114. Sales this year divided by company and competitor's sales this year
115. Marketing contribution divided by marketing assets
116. Marketing costs divided by sales
117. Sales divided by marketing assets
118. Variable production costs divided by sales
119. Warehouse costs divided by sales
120. Advertising costs divided by sales
121. Distribution costs divided by sales
122. Selling costs divided by sales
123. Discounts divided by sales
124. Sales office costs divided by sales
125. Bad debts divided by sales
126. Variable production costs divided by sales
127. Finished goods stock divided by sales
128. Finished goods divided by sales
129. Selling and distribution vehicles divided by sales
130. Finished goods stock divided by average daily production and all costs of goods sold
131. Accounts receivable divided by average daily sales
132. Sales divided by number of orders
133. Sales office costs divided by number of orders
134. Debtors divided by total sales
135. Estimated variable contract costs divided by orders
136. Marketing costs divided by orders
137. Orders divided by quotations actually presented

138. Marketing costs divided by quotations
139. Orders divided by sales
140. Orders outstanding divided by average daily sales
141. Sales by representatives divided by total sales
142. Sales by agents divided by total sales
143. Selling office costs divided by sales dollars
144. Representatives' compensation and expenses divided by sales per representative
145. Agents' commissions divided by sales by agents
146. Representatives' compensation and expenses divided by number of calls made by representatives
147. Number of orders obtained by representatives divided by number of calls made by representatives
148. Sales by representatives divided by number of orders obtained

Ratio Comparison by Month, Quarter or Year

149. Warehouse costs
150. Distribution costs
151. Advertising costs
152. Selling costs
153. Discounts
154. Sales office costs
155. Bad debts
156. Warehouse costs divided by sales
157. Marketing costs divided by sales
158. Distribution costs divided by sales
159. Advertising costs divided by sales
160. Selling costs divided by sales
161. Discounts divided by sales
162. Sales office costs divided by sales
163. Bad debts divided by sales
164. Sales divided by number of orders or invoices
165. Sales office costs divided by the number of orders or invoices
166. Finished goods inventory divided by sales
167. Accounts receivable divided by average daily sales
168. Distribution costs divided by sales
169. Selling costs divided by sales
170. U.S. distribution sales divided by total sales
171. U.S. selling costs divided by U.S. sales
172. Export selling costs divided by export sales

9

HOW TO MEASURE SALES MANAGEMENT PERFORMANCE

Background Management Data

1. What is the company's sales volume for each of the past ten years?

2. Has this sales volume risen at least 50 percent in the last ten years? At least 25 percent in the last five years?

3. Adjusted for inflation, what is your "real" dollar volume increase?

4. What are the sales volume figures for the industry in which your company competes?

5. What is your company's share of this market? Does it follow industry trends? Is it increasing or decreasing?

6. Has your company had the function of sales analysis assigned to a specific person, who generates weekly data on sales?

7. Are your marketing and sales executives reacting appropriately to this information, bolstering sales strengths and correcting weaknesses?

8. Are your sales forecasts or projections realistic and attainable but reasonably ambitious and based on sound market research and analysis?

9. Are forecasts made for sales of each product category for each year? Are these forecasts developed at least two years ahead of announcement date? Do they measure units of sales as well as dollar volume?

10. Are the forecasts prepared in sufficient detail so that quantitative performance measures objectively may be placed against them?

11. Has a detailed sales analysis been made of your company's customers? Chief customers? Is this categorized in a useful manner as to requirements, characteristics, geographic locations, size or composition?

12. Has an equally detailed sales analysis been performed of your chief competitors' customers?

13. Do you have written analysis, including sales benefits, of your company's products? Is this in the hands of all salespeople? Does this include feature and use comparison, price comparison, delivery comparison or other pertinent sales points?

14. Is sales profitability measured in terms of salesperson, territory, individual customer as well as category of customer?

15. What is the average sales volume in dollar amounts for each salesperson?

16. How many calls does he or she make to achieve these sales? Overall, what is the ratio of sales calls to actual sales for the department?

17. What is your company's average cost of sales calls? What is the ratio of selling costs to sales volume?

18. What is the percentage difference between the highest-ranking and lowest-ranking salesperson measured in dollar volume of sales?

19. What is the average earnings of your salespeople?

20. Does your company have computer programming focused on sales analysis and performance measurement?

21. What is the average tenure of a salesperson in your company?

22. What is the distribution of age categories by division or department? Is the ratio balanced?

23. Do your salespeople routinely fill out their call reports? Is the information reported accurate and useful, and is it productively used?

24. Do you measure each salesperson's profitability? Each sales district or area's profitability?

25. Does management receive prompt and regular information on the status of current orders so that they can determine trends and make informed decisions to protect profitability?

26. Do you measure profitability for each customer?

27. Does management have a quick means of determining the effects of special promotions or price changes on sales volume or profitability?

28. Does management know quickly of any negative changes in sales volume or other deviations from projected or forecast sales?

29. Has the percentage of sales returns or customer adjustments changed negatively in the past several years? If so, why?

30. Are sales correlated with production and inventories?

31. For each salesperson, customer, district or market, does management have the "marginal" income (net sales minus all direct costs)?

32. Is market research done on a continuous rather than on a "one shot" basis?

33. What percentage of your gross profit comes from the sale of spare parts?

34. Does what your customers think, in terms of your product, get back via your salespeople to your marketing, engineering, production or other departments?

35. Do you have a quick means to learn from customers about fast- or slow-moving items?

Sales Management Performance Objectives

36. Increase new orders by N percent or N dollars.

37. Increase prices by N percent no later than D date.

38. Establish new distribution channel by D date to reduce costs by N percent or N dollars and to increase sales by N percent or N dollars.

39. Achieve advertising expense ratio to sales of N percent.

40. Install new quota program by D date for N salespeople.

41. Allocate N advertising dollars from A channel to B channel.

42. Install new incentive program by D date for N personel to reduce compensation-to-sales ratio from N percent to N percent.

Sales Management Measurements and Factors

43. Sales expense divided by sales revenue.

44. Advertising expense divided by sales revenue.

45. Sales force productivity:
   • Selling man-hours divided by dollars of sales
   • Number of units sold divided by man-weeks

46. Physical distribution cost per unit.

47. Service expense ratio: repair costs (or, R&A) divided by sales dollars.

48. Average sales dollars divided by orders.

49. Annual sales volume, divided by major time periods or product groups.

50. Selling profit or target margin to be obtained

51. Territory expense and local funds for selling programs and customer support

52. Other financial standards:
   • average account receivables outstanding
   • value of inventory

53. Sales accomplishments:
- new customers gained
- training programs conducted
- new products introduced.

Sales Performance Improvement Objectives

54. Change price leads—up or down.

55. Add new products to the line.

56. Eliminate low-volume or low-profit products.

57. Increase or decrease the number of salespeople.

58. Expand or contract geographical sales areas.

59. Change credit or collection policies.

60. Change advertising and promotion priorities—up, down or modify.

61. Change packaging and label design.

62. Change methods of distribution.

63. Change the original structure of the sales direction and supervision.

64. Eliminate peaks and valleys in the sales curve.

65. Develop new markets or applications.

66. Improve motivation of salespeople to increase productivity.

67. Combine small shipments to gain lower freight rates for larger volumes.

68. Raise or lower the amount of customer service work performed by sales people.

Field Sales Management Objectives

69. Sales quotas are set for each salesperson and checked every X days.

70. Quotas have been negotiated in advance with individual sales-people and compensation is tied to these.

71. Compensation programs take into account the profitability of sales rather than sales volume alone.

72. The sales management's time is spent on managing the sales force and engineering sales rather than participating in direct selling.

73. Sales management receives data on accounts receivable with zero current balance for X days.

74. Corrective action is taken within N days on delinquent accounts.

75. Factors behind the growth of certain accounts or the decline of other accounts are identified and corrective action is taken.

76. Sales territories and new markets are regularly evaluated and explored.

77. Sales force receives training in selling all products and product benefits.

78. Use of sales agents or selling through distributors is routinely explored. If they are used currently, management checks the profitability of these sales methods.

79. Sales people participate when sales call quotas and other sales data are decided upon.

80. Salespeople have firm instructions when possible variances under established prices or exceeding costs are considered.

81. Salespeople are called to meet on a regular basis. These meetings are informative, constructive and positive, resulting in open communication and mutual problem solving.

Sales Manager: Management Performance Objectives

82. Achieves annual sales quota in all areas within plus or minus X percent as shown in sales control reports comparing sales against quota. Above-average performance is shown by achieving sales more than X percent over quota for all markets.

83. Increases sales by at least X percent over the previous year in all markets as shown in sales control reports comparing current sales with sales of the same period the previous year. Above-average performance is demonstrated by increasing sales more than X percent in each market.

84. Does not exceed by more than X percent the allocated sales budget as shown in the sales control reports comparing current expenses with assigned budget. Above-standard performance is holding actual expenses to less than budgeted amount.

85. Achieves estimated quarterly gross and dollars contributions by plus or minus X percent as measured in quarterly sales control reports comparing gross and dollar totals with estimated amounts. Above-average performance is gross or dollar contributions X percent more than estimated.

86. Sales reflect overall trends of industrial indexes as well as company national averages as measured by monthly sales control reports which give company national averages as well as other published data for comparison. Above-average performance results from sales greater than national or company averages.

Sales Promotion Management Monitoring Objectives

87. Decisions on what, where and how to advertise are made after careful market study.

88. Sales promotion budgets, including advertising, are regularly provided.

89. Value analysis is performed to measure program effectiveness.

90. Sales department expenses have adhered to budget within X percent last year. During the last five years.

91. Advertising expenditures made by the outside agency are reviewed monthly to determine that billings reflect actual advertising that has been published or aired. Or that proper rate applications have been made and discounts, if applicable, applied on special "media" buys.

92. Invoices for time, printing or ad space are double-checked for accuracy.

93. The sales or technical literature adequately tells predetermined product or company benefits.

94. Checks have been made to determine that the company has been reimbursed for cooperative advertising. Ads are checked systematically to be certain advertising is run as claimed, and that reimbursements total the payments actually made.

95. A system is in effect so that amounts budgeted for programs that have been cut, tabled or changed are used to reduce the overall budget and not simply used for new, unauthorized or "extra" projects. There is no "slush" fund.

Sales Performance Measurements (Product Line, Division or Market)

(in dollar volume compared with projections)

96. This month

97. Current month last year

98. Current month for past N years

99. Total for year to date

100. Total for year to date last year

101. Total for year to date for last X years

102. Cumulative annual total this month

103. Cumulative annual total this month last year

104. Cumulative annual total this month for the last X years

105. Sales volumes in X product lines

106. Sales volumes in N price ranges

107. Sales volumes in X territories or districts

108. Dollar volumes for 100 or N salespeople

109. Number of sales calls for month

110. Number of sales calls averaged for each of 100 salespeople

111. Number of new customers or projects per salesperson

112. Sales calls per day, analyzed by high, medium and low rates of call

113. Number of orders per 100 calls

114. Number of orders per man-day

115. Average order size, in both dollars and units

116. Sales volume per salesperson-day, in dollars and units

Sales Management: Monitoring Objectives

117. All sources have been analyzed and utilized for sales leads

118. Inquiries are handled through an organized and effective system complete with monitoring of results.

119. The sales staff is trained in time management and planning techniques to save time and achieve greater productivity.

120. Sales promotions and product promotions are coordinated and timed to meet changing economic or market conditions.

121. New services, new emphasis or new products or pricing are considered and evaluated to increase sales.

122. The portion of market which provides the greatest new probability for increased sales has been identified, and steps for making inroads have been initiated.

123. The company has been surveyed within the last N months to determine it is competitive within the market for quality of product, type of product and services.

124. A specific, prioritized and quantitative plan has been developed to increase sales by X dollars by N date.

125. The current and planned company share of the market is known in relation to:

a. sales volume percentage
b. percentage of customers
c. customers per product
d. customers per district or area
e. customers per buyer category
f. customers per salesperson
g. profit ratio
h. customer turnover per
   district
   product
   salesperson

126. Sales volume goals have been established for major products within specified time periods. These are understood by all concerned, and these employees receive communications regularly on their progress toward meeting their goals.

127. The goals are only established after careful analysis of field estimates, data inputs and market estimates as well as determination on prevailing market conditions.

128. The selling profit has been defined in measurable terms for the sales force and they receive these data.

129. The sales force has an organized, systematic method of handling information so that prompt and accurate reporting of performance against goals occurs every N days.

130. Goals for market share or for percentage of distribution effectiveness have been established. Progress is accurately measured and communicated.

131. Objectives for new customers to be gained have been established for present markets.

132. The specific results to be achieved in the sales of new products have been clearly defined in writing.

133. Annual goals have been set for sales to key customers and prospects.

134. All tasks which involve the sales force, but which do not have to do directly with selling, have been identified and defined in writing. The results to be obtained from these tasks have been identified and made clear.

135. A plan complete with timetable has been established for an expansion of the sales force into new markets.

136. The department has an up-to-date map which shows at a glance the sales coverage plan.

137. Geographic sales objectives have been summarized by showing sales or profit goals according to significant areas, products, or time periods.

138. All present market segments have been analyzed and data on types of customers and prospects have been extracted so that the sales force may proceed to call on them.

139. The outer boundary of the geographical area that is to be in the sales plan has been defined and communicated.

140. All sales made to each customer are systematically and quickly reported to management. Profit is reported along with sales.

141. The department regularly prepares consolidated customer lists, ranking the accounts in order of sales, the profits earned by the company, and the total potential yearly requirements of the customer.

142. Customers have been grouped according to key sales areas or market segments and information has been extracted on the sales revenue and profit potential for each major category.

143. An organized procedure is used for collecting and recording information about new account propsects in the market segment.

Monitoring Objectives Against Performance

144. Have standards been developed and is information routinely processed on key, regular as well as unprofitable customers? Have accounts been classified accordingly?

145. Do reports identify accounts that have stopped buying, according to standards, as either a "lost customer" or still a "potential customer?"

146. Does sales routinely receive information from other corporate departments about prospective customers?

147. Has a system been developed and put in operation so that salespeople can rate prospects according to their value to the company as well as the probability of selling to them? Is a list of major prospects kept current?

148. Are regular reevaluations made to determine which former customers can realistically be expected to buy again? Is an up-to-date list circulated?

149. Has the basic sales coverage plan been coordinated fully with the company's marketing strategy, with guidelines established and communicated to indicate the sales volume projected for each major category of customer?

150. Have call frequency patterns been determined in instances where it seems logical to do so to help guide the salesman's efforts?

151. Is a review of current major market segments and of sales coverage routinely made and are efforts designed or modified to fit existing sales situations?

152. Is the effort of sales coverage based on the value of sales potential as well as the difficulty of the undertaking? Do salespeople call on predetermined accounts with increased frequency so as to maximize impact on prioritized customers?

153. Is the sales information system streamlined but effective so the salesperson is not burdened with unnecessary paperwork? Does any salesperson spend more than N minutes per day on "paperwork?" Are results summarized daily for management?

154. Are the capabilities of marketing organizations, manufacturer's agents or outside salespeople analyzed and employed when the company can use them to best advantage?

155. Are sales forces centered according to potential market opportunities and not according to plant locations, past organizational arrangements, convenience or geography?

156. Have all alternatives for setting up the sales force for maximum potential been analyzed?

157. Has the work performed by senior salespeople handling the major volumes and profits to the company been analyzed so that some of their less important tasks can be performed by less experienced, and less costly, people? Can the senior force's time be better utilized?

158. Have actual total selling hours of each salesperson been computed by analyzing his or her major activities per year?

159. Have the procedures for developing new accounts been established and communicated and has the percentage of selling time been determined?

160. Has selling time needed to cover various customer groups been established by using analysis of previous sales?

161. Has the division of a salesperson's annual selling time been calculated, and is it realistic for this person to handle present customers, new accounts, as well as deal with new opportunities and unplanned events and crises? Is the person, on the other hand, underutilized?

162. Have the selling time and the selling need calculations been analyzed to estimate the number of salespeople needed?

163. Has the optimal size of the sales force been determined based on market potential analysis?

164. Has geographic coverage been analyzed to determine sales coverage needs?

165. Has incremental sales information been developed with the aid of the accounting department? Has the break-even point been established for existing customers and determinations made on what incremental additions will specifically accomplish?

166. Have data for several different sizes of sales forces been compared and analyzed for cost and profitability to the company?

167. Has a trial sales budget been developed and tested against inputs and ratios before being put into effect as a final sales budget?

168. Has the tentative sales budget been reviewed by other concerned departments, including marketing, and has the budget been sent to management? Have their inputs been carefully considered and acted upon?

169. Are current and future manpower needs based on data and identified trends, been analyzed? Have the number and type of replacements needed in the next year been anticipated? Two years from now? Five?

170. Have non-advertising recruiting techniques for new salespeople been analyzed and most effective ways utilized? Are they functional so that sales routinely receives a steady flow of applicants?

171. Do company suppliers, peer groups, professional organizations and customers know of sales manpower needs, and do they routinely send candidates? How many candidates were received via this route last year?

172. Are all interviews for sales candidates handled through a predetermined system so that a unified overall impression can be gained by qualified people within the department?

173. Do all likely candidates receive a thorough check of past employment and recorded education? Is all information verified, including direct checks with previous employers? Does the person who is making the hiring decision do the direct checking by telephone interview?

174. Is sales aptitude testing used for each sales applicant as a guide to an applicant's potential sales performance? Do correlary statistics provide "weight" for the use of this test?

175. Does the company have an open system of job posting so that all employees can have a chance at sales vacancies? Does the company try to fill sales vacancies, when possible, from within the organization, particularly with people who have the aptitude for selling and want to do so?

176. Does each new employee or person new in a position receive an individual sales training program which is positive in nature and which involves him or her directly?

177. Is each person in a new sales job told exactly what he or she is expected to do in terms of results to be achieved? Is agreement reached on job standards and measurements? Is emphasis placed on an employee's achieving certain results, rather than performing "activities?"

178. If a person fails to perform a sales job that is up to pre-agreed standards, is this person told about specific job deficiencies so that the person may correct the problem? A firing or reassignment never comes as a "surprise."

179. Are basic sales skills needed for each sales position analyzed and taught through systematic training classes, including those coordinated by outside sales consultants?

180. Do basic sales skills include product knowledge, how to convert product features into customer benefits, how to analyze customer needs, and a full range of basic technical information, as well as how to convert it into applicable sales communication?

181. Does each salesperson know how to plan and make a sales call in terms of the basic components of a call? Do these include: *basic psychology* of selling, *planning* the call and *pre-approach* details including sales aids or data; the *approach*, including analysis of what way the salesperson will begin the sales call in the presence of the customer; the economical *presentation* of the sales material based on customer needs; the *sales close*, in which the salesperson asks for the order and other sales techniques, including *how to handle objections*? If needed, has an outside consultant been hired to upgrade the sales staff in these sales skill basics?

182. Does each salesperson have available various leave-behind communications materials, including form letters for pre-call greetings, post-call thanks, brochures, booklets, flip charts and, if appropriate, customer catalogs?

183. Does each salesperson, as well as sales management, analyze his or her call results periodically to improve performance?

184. Have all selling aids been developed professionally to meet specific selling objectives? Do standards for sales aids include clarity of explanation, development of a single "theme" and production of high quality? Are these reviewed every N months for effectiveness, pertinence, timeliness and, when needed, upgraded?

185. Is every selling aid tested prior to production by representatives of both the best and the weakest salespeople, as well as distributors, suppliers and customers?

186. Are all sales campaigns coordinated and timed to provide salespeople with a concentrated, planned method of achieving major selling goals?

187. Does the sales force know that measements for appraising performance are quantitative, unified and objective? Is emphasis on achieving goals? Is the sales environment a positive one with good communications, and are achievements reinforced by financial and other rewards?

188. Does each sales area know the goals and objectives the company wants it to achieve? Has it had input into the goals it is to achieve, and does it receive communication every N days so that it may appraise itself and make corrections as needed?

189. Do quantitative surveys show that the sales force feels it is used to capacity and that it has inputs into the establishment of the goals it is expected to achieve?

190. Are appraisals honest and open? Does each person know where he or she stands, and do they either perform to expected and predetermined standards of performance, receive training to meet these standards or are they released from the sales force? Does the company not retain beyond N days salespeople who do not perform to predetermined standards of performance over a period of N months?

191. Is a major means of communications in the sales force regularly scheduled meetings with predetermined and preprinted agendas? Has each meeting clear objectives, and is every person attending expected to have inputs? Are the meetings positive?

192. Are outside consultants regularly employed for training of sales force supervisors and managers to bring the personnel to desired levels of performance? Has the performance of outside consultants been checked and analyzed as to results obtained by the people they train? Is all training results-oriented to established needs with a "no-nonsense" approach? Do programs and specific trainers have a history of proven success for similar sales forces?

193. Are sales compensations attracting and retaining the sales force the company desires? Was the sales compensation plan arrived at after a study of possible applicable plans as the best alternative for the company? Or was it merely inherited or adapted from another company?

194. Are compensation plans explained to each salesperson, the results understood fully, and measurable by a reporting system used by the salesperson every N days? Are no rewards whatever given for personality traits? Are there no "Santa Claus" benevolences? Are all income or bonuses earned by strict adherence to predetermined standards?

195. Does the sales force know how to increase each individual is compensation based on individual, specific sales results?

196. Has each salesperson a specific set of goals with appropriate personal planning to earn compensation in increasing amounts? Does he or she receive regular, punctual feedback every N days on how well these goals are being achieved?

197. Is all regular compensation directly tied to individual, not group, performance?

198. Do salespeople participate in regularly scheduled short-term, company-wide incentive plans and sales contests? Do contests reward only achievement of results?

199. Do contests generate enthusiasm for rewards and recognition by the sales force? Does the sales force participate in aspects of the planning of these contests within overall company goals? Do the contests produce the short-term results for which they were designed? What about the long-range effect of contests—does production "peak" during the contest and then slump so much after that the net effect is neutralized?

10

HOW TO MEASURE ENGINEERING RESEARCH AND DEVELOPMENT MANAGEMENT PERFORMANCE

Management Background Data

1. Is R & D formally structured as a department with clear responsibilities spelled out on an organizational chart?

2. Does every person have a clear description of project objectives, responsibilities and timetables?

3. Does R & D work under a budget system for a projected series of objectives and does it manage itself so well as to adhere to the budget, plus or minus N percent?

4. Does R & D operate under a body of well-considered corporate information and values within which parameters are clearly defined?

5. Has an outside study been made within the past two years to determine if R & D may be organized for more bottom-line effectiveness? Past five years?

6. Are R & D's efforts centered upon results measurably of value to the company's profitability?

7. For the past operating year, what was your total R & D cost:
- personnel
- space
- equipment
- all others

8. What percentage is the above in comparison with costs of the previous year? Two years ago? Five?

9. Do R & D costs outweigh their company "profit" contributions?

10. In the past operating year, what is R & D's quantified record of:
- product improvement
- new products
- new materials
- process improvements
- cost-cutting procedures
- other results

11. How does this record compare with two years ago? Five years ago? In comparison with your next leading competitor?

12. Are reports developed weekly for all objectives and major projects so that progress on R & D's efforts may be evaluated?

13. Does R & D have a priority system set by management as an aid in scheduling? Is this regularly reviewed?

14. Does R & D planning anticipate workloads so that "bottlenecks" can be avoided?

15. Are manpower imbalances forecast in advance so that they can be avoided?

16. Is unnecessary or redundant work or are time commitments screened out through work authorization systems?

17. What is the percent of total man-hours of R & D overtime during the past year? Over the past two years? Is it more than 10 percent?

18. What is the percent of total man-hours actually worked on scheduled assignments? Is it less than 90 percent?

19. Does R & D answer to a standards team concerned overall with product design, materials, improvements or other efforts?

20. Do R & D managers have specific corporate "bottom-line" responsibilities which they appreciate and understand so that they are not so deeply involved in the esoterics of design or research detail that they waste time or effort? Do they receive regular feedback on their results as measured against specific objectives?

21. What is the R & D percentage of total cost to gross sales (profit contribution) this last year? The last two years? Five years?

22. Has a "profit contribution" of R & D been specified and routinely measured?

Research and Development Management Objectives

23. Reduce costs of X product by N percent by N date.

24. Complete development of Y product by N date in conformance with approved product plan specifications.

25. Apportion research expenses on the basis of N percent basic and N percent applied.

26. While maintaining new product development and existing services, reduce the budget as a percentage of net sales from N to N percent in the new N-year profit plan.

27. Provide value analysis plan within parameters of X considerations for Engineering Section E prior to N date.

28. Reduce the pay-out time of research investment from current N years to N years.

29. Generate X new product introductions in the next N years so that the company may continue its market position as a leading competitor.

30. Intensify research capabilities in project Y by hiring N PhD's with suitable backgrounds and proven capabilities.

31. Design and develop prototype X in N months within a cost of N dollars utilizing only internal capabilities.

32. Deliver to marketing N new products within N months with projected sales of not less than N million dollars.

33. Concentrate R & D's ratio of feasible marketing ideas to actual products marketed from N to N within the next N months.

34. Complete plans, costs and schedule for N months for X project and secure approval of Department X by N date.

35. Complete PERT layout for Project X within the pre–budgetary planning cycle.

36. Develop N new products within product line X for introduction by N date for N patentable concepts for use in entering X, Y, and Z markets.

37. Complete patent search and related information by N date for N patentable concepts for use in entering X, Y and Z markets.

Research and Development Administrative Management Job Elements

38. Provide work plans and project schedules.

39. Develop work progress and cost controls.

40. Provide adequate physical facilities and equipment.

41. Develop information that can be used to standardize costs.

42. Relate company goals and objectives to research and engineering objectives.

43. Provide a competent staff to achieve the objectives.

44. Provide a program for training and upgrading the staff.

Research and Development Management Performance and Productivity Improvement Measures

45. Does R & D regularly make use of computer time on its various projects?

46. Does R & D maintain accurate and detailed records of personnel and projects along with costs?

47. Have the accuracy and detail on projects within the last year been satisfactory?

48. Do systems exist for the revising of major projects?

49. Are project estimates, covering time, costs and completion dates, provided for all identifiable projects?

50. Are lines of authority detailed for all functions and the approving of budgets?

51. Are internal and outside suppliers' work charges accumulated individually and by individual project by accounting?

52. Are schedules coordinated with other applicable departments?

53. Is scheduling done by a manager other than the one responsible for the completion of the project?

54. Is a breakdown made weekly of the department's use of man-hours as to work in progress and man-hours behind in reaching objective or ahead of objective?

55. Is there standardization of design details and related forms as well as filing and distribution?

56. Is a regular "security" system in effect on new projects or concepts? Has it been tested?

57. Is there a task force which routinely uses value analysis to arrive at product costs and features? Is analysis used to determine cost reductions or method improvements?

58. Are certain costs of R & D charged back to the divisions which order certain projects?

59. Is there a quantified review of proposed projects to determine profitability, features, time allocated, materials, etc.?

60. Are recurring problems identified and analyzed? Or do the same basic problems keep cropping up?

61. Does R & D maintain a technical library, under skilled supervision, which can be used for reference by non–R & D personnel?

62. Is vendor and other reference material on microfilm or easily used?

63. Is all of R & D in one location and in a planned work environment with adequate support staff, space and equipment?

64. Does R & D have adequate conference space, training rooms, etc.?

65. Is work organized along project lines, with specific responsibilities? (Or is R & D organized along traditional company patterns or hierarchies?)

66. Do specialists have sufficient clerical or support staff so that they can concentrate mainly on corporate problem-solving or objectives? Is what they do approved in advance and checked against overall corporate needs?

67. If many subspeciality or narrow technical groups are utilized, is their specialty justified?

68. Is routine review made of workloads and purposes for the purpose of determining new priorities, directions or improvements?

69. Are responsibilities and authorities the result of logical analysis or traditional supervisory methods?

70. What is the ratio of:
   - managers to employees?
   - technical to nontechnical personnel?
   - postgraduate to graduate or nongraduate personnel?
   - support or clerical staff to technical staff?

71. Is a system functional to test suggestions from other departments regarding procedural or technical problems?

72. Are new ideas welcomed and acted upon with adequate two-way communications dispatched with timeliness?

73. Has R & D management undertaken broad managerial training? Does the department have formal training and orientation for new personnel?

74. What is the turnover for technical personnel? Is it higher or lower than industry or corporate norms?

75. What is the correlation between turnover and corporate financial programs? Is the company program substandard?

76. Does a career enhancement program allow R & D personnel to broaden or upgrade their technical as well as managerial skills with company aid?

11

HOW TO MEASURE
PURCHASING MANAGEMENT
PERFORMANCE

Management Background Data

1. What is the gross dollar value of all purchases made this past fiscal year?

2. What is the breakdown of these purchases in terms of primary categories, such as materials, components, labor, vendors or other services?

3. What percentage of all company purchases are actually handled by the purchasing department (not just approved)?

4. What are the main categories of purchases? What percentage are these of the total? Which comprise 80 percent of total purchases?

5. Does a cost analysis performed during the past year show that company purchases are above or lower than supplier "norms" of cost?

6. Are purchases, in excess of N dollars, made after three competitive bids are received—or are bids always from the same supplier? What purchases are from the same vendor?

7. What is the ratio of company costs to purchased items? Percentage of purchases to sales volume? Are these showing change?

8. What percentage of purchase requisitions are marked "rush," or "ship as soon as possible" or otherwise indicate a need for other-than-normal haste? What does an analysis show of pricing on these orders?

9. What percent of orders in each category are "exceptions" to the lowest bid which still meets order standards?

10. What percentage of orders are shipped by the most economical method? What percent by the most expeditious?

11. What percent of orders receive a verification of transportation allowances?

12. What percent of orders have a price variance from original requisitions?

13. Is a continual quality control analysis performed as a means of determining purchasing's performance?

14. What percentage of all company orders are *not* requisitioned through formal purchase orders and ordered through purchasing? Does an analysis of these purchases show a quantifiable trend? How many major purchases have been made outside the prescribed company purchasing system?

15. What percentage of mail is not metered? What percent of metered mail is "personal?"

16. What percent of all material is classified as "scrap" or "seconds"? Has this changed in the last N months? What percentage of this is sold by competitive bid to different vendors?

17. What percent of all orders reflect a "cash discount" or "early payment" discount? Of these, what percent has purchasing actually availed itself of? What percent were lost—and for what reason?

18. What percentage of orders in connection with predetermined inventory levels result in lower-than-desired levels? Higher levels? On-target levels?

19. What percentage of applicable purchasing functions and information have been adapted to electronic data processing?

20. What areas or functions should be computerized?

21. What percentage of major vendors have been analyzed within the past year for value studies, for pricing or for comparisons with other possible suppliers?

22. Have outside vendors or services been studied with the aim of cutting these costs by duplicating their service or product internally? What percentage of "outside" buys have been transferred in this manner?

23. What percentage of all purchases conform to written company purchasing guidelines?

24. What percentage of company purchases are made on the basis of fully evaluated and tested bids?

25. What number of major purchases are negotiated in person by purchasing management with suppliers? What percentage of all purchases does the negotiated total represent?

26. Are there guidelines for "small" purchases—and has an analysis of purchases made outside the purchasing department confirmed that purchases fall within established guidelines as to price and value?

27. What percentage of all orders are without purchasing's input for material selection, specifications or supplier?

28. What percent of all deliveries are to a centralized receiving location? What percent go directly to the departments or areas that are to use the purchases? (If direct delivery to other than purchasing, what system checks out the purchases?)

Objectives for Purchasing Management

29. Use value analysis to determine less expensive components or materials which may be substituted for more expensive ones.

30. Lower inventory levels by getting more frequent deliveries.

31. Institute incoming quality control.

32. Combine small lot purchases into large volume company-wide purchases.

33. Standardize as much as possible to reduce number of brands and types of the same items.

34. Reduce time-cycle between purchase and delivery.

Objectives for Purchasing Management Performance Improvement

35. Analyze changes in the organization to upgrade the role of purchasing.

36. Change suppliers

37. Centralize or decentralize purchasing authority.

Purchasing Management Plan of Action Elements

38. Determine alternatives as to:
- sources of supply
- timing of purchases
- quality
- service obtained

39. Plan the purchasing forecast and schedule

40. Set objectives.

41. Formulate plans to reach objectives.

Responsibilities of Purchasing Management

42. Purchase materials at the lowest bid cost to the standards set for quality and service.

43. Perform value analysis and cost analysis on purchases of materials.

44. Maintain continuity of supply to support company production with a minimum investment in materials.

45. Communicate information on material or supplier developments which require management decision on corporate profitability, productivity or performance.

46. Maintain and analyze records pertaining to all purchases, including:
- price records
- purchase records
- specification files
- catalog files
- data on maximum and minimum stock levels for ordering as well as consumption patterns and trends
- vendor records
- records of transport companies and freight rates.

47. Analyze requisitons for the following conformances:
- specifications
- quantity
- price
- delivery dates
- issuing authority
- duplication of requisition with stock already on hand.

48. Receive vendor's bids within N days. Though some purchases may be done under a master contract, purchasing usually requires at least three competitive bids. Specifications are written so that vendors can bid on them precisely.

49. Evaluate vendors and bids:
- Get best possible price and performance on the basis of bids submitted, following up on the most promising bids by assembling facts and statistics and using these for final negotiations.
- Make determination of factors other than initial costs alone, such as total costs, related costs, status of vendor and vendor's rating and past history as to reliability and performance. Considerations are given to a vendor's technical competence, maintenance of delivery dates, and overall stability.
- Inspect major supplier's plants and interview key managers involved in product to get data "in person" so as to make an informed purchasing decision.

50. Evaluate best purchasing plan for company:
- Long term or "master contract," which locks in one supplier but to preset standards and with a discount benefit. This avoids costs of frequent small orders.
- One-time only, strictly competitive bid from three sources, with specifications rigidly defined with final selection on the basis of lowest bidder who can meet specifications.

51. Make determinations on legal or other considerations, including trade regulation laws, adherance to codes, product liability considerations, nonperformance or warranties.

52. Schedule purchases, issue purchase orders, coordinate effort with other departments.

53. Check materials for specification conformance, verify invoice.

54. Make adjustments with vendors for nonconformance to specifications, defective materials or rejects.

55. Help determine standards and specifications for ongoing as well as new product purchases which will affect costs, prices or other value considerations.

Managerial Decision Making Milestones for Performance Testing of New Purchased Items

56. Purchasing begins cycle by obtaining all data about new purchases, including prices, specifications and samples.

57. Engineering performance tests samples under laboratory and other conditions, reporting results as well as making recommendations.

58. Purchasing then performs a value analysis on the new purchase, compares new source with present supplier and, in turn, makes recommendation.

59. Other applicable departments review engineering and purchasing's tests, performance analysis and value analysis, and react on recommendations.

60. Production checks production efficiency by testing a sample in regular operation and reports on results.

61. Engineering initiates an overall performance evaluation by incorporating a purchase sample into the regular company product. Reports recommendations.

62. Sales maintains a check on customer acceptance through the sales process and notes overall sales trends with new product. Makes recommendations.

63. Purchasing gathers reports and makes proposal to purchase in quantity. Receives concurrence of decision makers.

64. Purchasing receives final authorization to purchase in quantity. It issues purchase order, complete with standards, dates, prices and other data to complete the transaction.

Purchasing Management Performance Measurements

65. Dollars of purchases divided by gross sales

66. Buying costs divided by purchase dollars

67. Buying costs divided by number of purchases

68. Dollars of purchases divided by number of purchases

69. Percentage of purchases which are rejected

70. Value of rejects and monetary adjustments divided by purchases

71. Percentage of shortages in scheduled production goods

72. Value of orders overdue divided by the average daily value of purchases

73. Value of orders outstanding divided by the average daily value of purchases

74. Purchases from each vendor divided by total purchases

75. Price variances divided by budgeted purchases

76. Inventory as a percentage of production

77. Inventory as a percentage of sales

78. Average costs of a requisition

79. Labor costs of a requisition

80. Average lead time

81. Flow time from request for a purchase to the issuance of the purchase order

82. Number of requisitions per month in comparison with forecast

83. Number of requisitions in comparison with Purchasing's time, postage costs, travel and freight

84. Vendor's performance compared against time, quality and costs

85. Buying contribution divided by buying assets (Buying contribution is the sales value of the production from which purchases and buying costs have been subtracted; buying assets consists of raw materials, components, etc., less credits)

Monitoring Objectives for Purchasing Management

86. Vendors' and suppliers' on-time performance, quality performance and standards conformance are analyzed at least quarterly and the results are issued to all applicable company staff.

87. Waiting time for "normal" requisition to an approved supplier with an ongoing, acceptable bid does not exceed N hours.

88. Market conditions, trends and forecasts which impact upon the price the company pays for materials or components are analyzed weekly and prompt action is taken for needed "buys."

89. A purchasing "Task Team" continuously analyzes purchasing and materials handling procedures to determine the most effective and efficient purchasing and handling. It comes forth with at least one new procedure every N months.

90. Once a month, one manager's task is to gather data on the routing of N shipments to determine if the most economical routes and methods have been used.

91. Purchasing has a coordinated plan with inventory control and production planning so that systematic inventory reorder points are known and acted upon, and the decision for necessary lead time has already been made. Inventory "markers" are in use.

92. Purchasing forms part of a "Task Team" with production engineering, etc., to conduct monthly studies on material value analysis, new materials or components or other areas of profitability to the company.

93. Purchasing has developed a system of objectives for its performance. Goals are set and managers evaluated against their accomplishment of these goals. Managers who exceed their negotiated goals are rewarded.

94. Purchasing routinely advises other departments of its needs for lead time so that engineering, material, or other changes will be anticipated and the company will not suffer from overbuying or untimeliness and obsolescence of inventory will be minimized.

95. Purchasing policies have been developed and communicated in writing to all departments and company areas.

96. Purchasing maintains current documentation of its procedures and systems. Only current copies are in the hands of users, and each copy is "sunset" dated with the notation: "This information is out of date: 'N date.' "

97. Procedures covered in purchasing's documentation include all of the following:
- standard purchasing forms, reports and files to be used for categories of requisitions
- written information on how to use forms, with standards for use of forms as well as goals and objectives
- how to requisition materials through purchasing
- procedures and responsibilities, including department signatures required and authorizations necessary
- standards to be met in purchases directly from a local supplier (including maximum dollar amount)
- blanket purchase orders, "Master Contracts," or long-term purchase arrangements with specific suppliers
- Interlocational or interdivisional purchases requirements
- data on how vendor evaluations and standards are established and how their performance is monitored
- governmental or legal considerations, including trade regulations, commercial codes, warranties, product liability considerations and nonperformance

98. Purchasing has a departmental organizational chart which shows staff positions and responsibilities and which identifies relationships.

99. No purchases beyond X dollars for N time period are made outside purchasing.

100. All pertinent data for purchasing are processed by computer.

101. Alternatives for restructuring purchasing have been considered after an analysis of purchasing's operations, performance and structure has been made.

102. Undelivered orders from vendors are canceled and replaced with new purchase orders after N hours.

103. Primary accounting functions are not performed by purchasing.

104. An approved vendor list has been compiled and distributed. Conformance is monitored.

105. Vendor selection is performed by the purchasing department. Selection is consistent with established performance standards and value analysis.

106. Prioritized deliveries which are late in being received are given special expedition or treatment. Followups are initiated routinely to prevent future problems.

107. A system is in effect so that those purchases delivered to separate work stations are checked and results are reported to purchasing.

108. Blanket purchase orders are provided for small unit items below N dollars total which are commonly used by many departments. These P.O.'s are monitored every N days.

109. Separate responsibilities are identified so that one individual is accountable for an entire purchase from beginning to end.

110. Exceptions to "lowest bid" policies are checked for results achieved and exceptions are controlled, based on these data.

111. Purchasing requisitions are sequentially numbered; and items are used and distributed as needed.

112. Employees who make requisitions have training in making purchases and have adequate information to make systematic no-nonsense decisions.

113. Price is included in the purchase order and does not exceed that quoted.

114. All factors, including delivery costs, distance, time, reliability, past consistency to standards, etc., are considered in the evaluation of competitive bids.

115. The company policy has been established and communicated toward vendor gifts or considerations of any sort to company purchasing personnel or departmental "buyers." No company individual may receive gifts, meals, or other considerations valued at more than N dollars per item.

116. Company policy identifies areas of possible conflict of interest between employees and company vendors. A special "task team" investigates reported cases monthly and violators are held accountable for situations which have arisen.

117. Accounting routinely checks invoices against receiving reports and inspection reports against purchase orders.

118. One person is accountable monthly to check all pertinent information on invoices, including freight charges, prices and extensions.

119. Prenumbered receiving reports with an adequate number of duplicate copies are used by appropriate divisions in their purchases.

120. Purchasing has the responsibility to sell surplus materials, obsolete items or "scrap." Clear standards as to what constitutes any of the above items have been formulated.

121. One person is charged with making a determination as to what is and what is not scrap, surplus or obsolete items or materials. Shipments are checked and detailed records are kept.

122. Surplus, obsolete materials or scrap items are sold on the basis of competitive bids every N months. Bidders vary, and the same companies do not routinely buy items at their offered bid.

123. Major vendors have been analyzed for their potential as company customers.

124. Purchasing does business with a diversity of suppliers so that the flow of materials and components to the company will continue in the event of a strike or problem with any one supplier.

125. Purchasing operates under the philosophy that most companies pay far too much for materials, goods and services, but that this particular company is the exception to the rule.

12

HOW TO MEASURE PRODUCTION PLANNING AND CONTROL MANAGEMENT PERFORMANCE

Background Data for Management

1. Are there regular workload reports as well as machine and manpower forecasts? How accurate are they?

2. Do all work stations have written standards of performance? If not, would these enhance performance?

3. Can exact status of any order be reported immediately?

4. Does Production Planning and Control issue a master schedule with all production assignments and time allocations?

5. What deviation does actual production take in comparison with the planned schedule?

6. What percentage of all orders are shipped as promised or planned?

7. Are manufacturing facilities scheduled for maximum utilization?

8. What percentage of overtime is attributable to production planning and control's scheduling?

9. Does each staff member have at least three improvement objectives for the next year?

10. What are the major order timetables, costs and quality standards for the past year? Have each of these categories been met? What are the variances in terms of percentages?

11. Are reports of performance against plans received by applicable managers within three days of the report period?

Production Planning and Control Management Objectives

12. The cost, quality and time schedule for each manufacturing unit will not exceed schedules by N percent

13. At least N percent will be earned on the assets employed to manufacture each product.

14. The cost of consumable supplies in comparison with the cost of production materials will not exceed N percent.

15. The total cost of parts and materials will not exceed N percent of product cost.

16. The master production plan will be submitted by N date.

17. All employees have production standards which they understand and are evaluated upon.

18. No operator will lose more than N minutes in a work week because of time spent locating materials assigned to his or her work station.

19. Work areas will receive work orders N days or N hours in advance of scheduled work.

20. Actual shipments of orders will occur according to schedule in N percent of all shipments.

21. Production Planning and Control can identify and report on the status of any order or work in progress within N minutes.

22. Overtime will be reduced by N dollars for N month by scheduling X work over work stations A, B and C.

23. Turnover of parts and materials is at least N percent each year.

24. All pertinent data for Production Planning and Control management are being processed by computer.

25. The costs of inventories of raw goods will be reduced by N percent during the fiscal year.

26. Cost improvement programming is begun in at least N work stations during N year.

27. Each manufacturing station will be audited every N months to determine overall efficiency and effectiveness.

Production Planning and Control Management Job Responsibilities

28. Assigns work to available production equipment and facilities so as to achieve schedule production within plus or minus N percent per time period. Work meets preset quality standards within N percent of predetermined costs.

29. Production meets all delivery schedules within plus or minus N percent.

30. Schedules manufacturing facilities for at least N percent of capacity to meet sales forecasts or customer orders.

31. Is knowledgeable at all times about the status of all orders as well as the levels of inventories and parts to be used so that plant capacity may be used to optimum advantage.

Production and Planning Management Productivity Improvement Measures

32. All inputs are into the EDP system for a daily status report of all projects, inventories and priorities within N minutes after each shift.

33. Starting time on each shop operation begins within N minutes of the scheduled time. If deviations occur beyond N minutes, an analysis is completed and adjustments made.

34. Every N days, Production Planning and Control compares its operating results and performance against standards, budgets and procedures. It issues quantitative reports to applicable management.

35. Task teams continually analyze Production Planning and Control's organization, planning and standards to recommend at least N changes every N days to increase effectiveness.

36. Master scheduling records, reporting systems and orders are analyzed every N days; trends are noted and deficiencies corrected.

37. A system of order and delay order reports is in use.

38. Production schedules are checked through the use of reporting systems distributed every N hours.

39. Evaluation occurs within N hours of receipt of incoming data to assess progress and to coordinate production with other schedules.

40. All operations have a documentation of work standards, and workers are held accountable for meeting standards.

41. Master schedules are checked every N hours against progress for all orders.

42. Each order goes out with a factory work order processing master and shop route sheet.

43. All jobs have actual time worked recorded on standard job time cards and factory work order cards.

44. Workload reports, manpower and machine requirements are forecast every N days.

45. Material control reports and production orders are distributed within N minutes of the start of the first shift.

46. A delayed order report is given to the plant manager no later than N A.M. each day.

47. Planning provides for production facilities to satisfy current product demands while maintaining proper inventory levels.

48. Before using outside suppliers, other operations of the company are checked to determine their ability to supply semifinished material or components for customer orders.

.**49.** Production Planning and Control is prepared to aid in the task of introducing N new products or changes in the line each year.

50. The unit issues timely studies on new developments which may impact on production or control. These analyses include pertinent insights into such areas as manufacturing engineering, manufacturing controls, facilities or traffic planning, construction, process engineering, maintenance, industrial engineering or manufacturing research.

51. Budget variances are analyzed and reported upon within N days after receipt of pertinent data. These variances are not expected to exceed N percent and in no more than N percent of all orders or projects. All losses will be clearly analyzed and reported in simple, everyday language so that any nonspecialized, reasonable person can understand exactly what the problem was.

52. Cost data are routinely prepared to support cost estimates for new projects.

53. Staff review is available to operating departments for short- and long-range planning.

54. Production Planning and Control takes part in a task team established company-wide standards of performance and systems for reporting as well as measuring accomplishments.

55. Essential control records and reports are maintained and distributed to cover not only current production loads, the status of current production orders, but schedule future loads.

56. The department issues weekly shipping performance reports, complete with scheduled timetables and actual shipping dates. Percentage of variances are included in the data.

57. The work flow of a manufacturing operation is shown with timetables on a master schedule to coordinate activities of all departments involved, from planning to manufacturing and, finally, shipping.

58. Factory work orders are coordinated with master schedules and proper accommodation given to lead time or priority rec,uirements.

59. Production Planning and Control schedules are attainable and realistic at all times although they may occasionally require some "stretching" to meet. The department commands a high degree of confidence and trust in its leadership and judgments.

60. The unit maintains coordination with other departments, including sales, and meets shipping dates within plus or minus N hours of promised times.

61. Work standards for each operation are reviewed at least every N months.

62. Errors in time cards do not exceed N percent.

63. The unit estimates plant capacity for each product every N months.

64. Stocks, materials or items which have been on hand for more than X months are reported.

65. Standards exist to classify materials and stocks as obsolete, and these are disposed of through set channels within N weeks after classification.

66. Certain materials or stocks are maintained as "backup" or "safety" stocks for X days or production in N categories.

67. Total inventory of materials and stocks in dollars do not exceed N dollar amount.

68. Inventory control procedures with automatic order points are operational and studied weekly for improvements, efficiencies and cost cutting.

69. Slow-moving or obsolete product items are noted and reported to appropriate managerial teams.

70. Study is made of the cause of work delays with appropriate data gathered so that such delays can be reduced from N hours to N hours during N month. Delays will not account for more than N percent of productive time per month.

71. A centralized Production Planning and Control will replace local planning and control by N date.

72. Lead time on stock X will be reduced by N days for N percent reduction of costs.

73. Production inventory will be decreased from X percent to X percent for all plants during N month.

74. New lead times and reorder levels for purchased materials are ordered when the level of business activity changes or when there are economic considerations which make a "speed-up" or "slowdown" desirable.

75. Long-range forecasting for at least N years out has been detailed so that the company's production facilities will be able to manufacture the volume and the kind of products the company is projected to market.

76. Production Planning and Control management has submitted programs to achieve company objectives for the next fiscal year and for each of the next N years.

77. Each company or plant receives a visit every N months for an on-site analysis of that facility's productivity, efficiency and performance.

78. Standard budget controls are in effect within other departments to ensure the approved use of funding.

79. Managers receive regular reports on operations for which they are responsible, and each manager is held accountable for specific results.

80. New sources of raw materials are continuously investigated.

81. The production cycle allows plant shutdowns for vacations or retooling to occur only during the lowest feasible phase of the company's annual demand cycle or during the annual plant shutdown.

82. Annual and quarterly production budgets are developed for each division or plant. These budgets indicate all the specifics forecast by marketing.

83. Each Production Planning and Control manager receives quantitative reports of his or her actual performance compared against negotiated goals and standards. Such report of accomplishments—or lack of them—comes regularly and quickly after a measured period ends. Rewards are provided for outstanding performance against goals and standards.

13

HOW TO MEASURE PRODUCTION MANAGEMENT PERFORMANCE

Background Data for Management

1. What is your plant's productivity:

- per dollar of plant investment?
- per dollar of wages?
- per employee?
- per man hour?

2. Has the ratio changed in the last year? Last three years? For the better—or worse?

3. How does your plant's performance measure up with your leading competitors? The industry in which you compete?

4. What is production management's degree of effectiveness as measured by the ratio of production costs divided by the sales value of production? Has this ratio changed in the past several years? What is the trend?

5. What is the correlation of inventory with sales levels? Is too much money tied up in inventory for too long a time?

6. What is the ratio of work farmed out to work produced by your production unit? Is that ratio increasing—along with your expenses?

7. What is the frequency rate of rescheduled production?

8. What percent of materials winds up as scrap or waste?

9. Have complaints been heard about designs that cannot be easily produced, designs which change production schedules, decisions that delay production or design changes which are "too frequent"?

10. Is the accounting department computing all costs of manufacturing and supplying these to production management on a weekly product-by-product basis? Is corrective action taken when facts contained in these reports indicate a need?

11. Are machines selected for certain production runs on the basis of best cost per unit and best machine speed? Have specific production standards been set and communicated for each machine and its use?

12. What is your actual material cost in terms of percent of production cost? What is the trend indicating?

Product Management Performance Improvement Goals

13. Determine optimum length and size of production run.

14. Arrange for the most efficient scheduling of production workers.

15. Change production locations.

16. Introduce process changes.

17. Establish optimum organization of production supervision.

18. Maintain proper balance between production scheduling and inventory levels.

19. Increase or decrease maintenance to match actual requirements.

20. Change plant layout and/or workflow.

21. Introduce or expand use of automated equipment.

22. Reduce fixed costs.

23. Alternatives:

- optimum inventory levels.
- adequacy of plant and equipment manufacturing facilities.
- raw materials and labor availability and utilization.
- length of production runs or season.
- annual production required.
- optimum location for manufacturing.

24. Raw materials forecast.

25. Production forecast and schedule.

26. Each manager assumes personal accountability in establishing and maintaining effective working relationships within production and with other divisions and departments.

27. Plans for reaching objectives.

Plant Production Manager Objectives

28. Complete construction and equipping of approved addition to new plant by N date within capital budget of N dollars and expense budget of N dollars.

29. Produce X number of Y products at N cost.

30. Install and have new equipment operational by N date within capital budget of N dollars and expense budget of N dollars.

31. Decrease the plant's quality reject rate from N percent to N percent by N date.

Overall Production Management Objectives

32. Any variances in excess of plus or minus N percent will be explained in writing within N hours of their occurrence.

33. No division will wait more than N working days for action on a production request.

34. Upgrade shipping performance to be on time during N year from N percent to N percent.

35. Reduce "down" time due to lack of parts or materials by N percent.

36. Raw material inventories will not exceed a ratio of N percent to the next quarter's volume as forecast.

37. Complete value analysis of Product X by N date.

38. Rearrange according to plan B the NY assembly line.

39. Study the effectiveness of the NY unit with the objective of reducing facilities and manpower now used to produce volume N or X product.

40. Reduce the accident frequency rate at Plant Y from N percent to N percent during N year.

41. N percent of all customer requests on order status will be answered within N hours after receipt of the request.

42. Back orders never exceed N percent of the plant's monthly shipments.

43. N percent of all orders will be shipped within N hours of their scheduled time.

44. Production is not late on more than N percent of its planned production.

45. Equipment "down" time because materials or components are not at the proper work stations or because of improper scheduling will not exceed N percent of the available machine hours.

46. All data on production are reviewed in depth at least once weekly. Data are distributed in written form to applicable other divisions and management teams.

47. New products and changes are brought into production without disrupting normal production flow and without incurring more than N hours of overtime.

48. Raw material stock for each product will fall to N days' supply at least once each month.

49. Quality control from Product X will be reduced in cost from N percent of sales to N percent during N date.

50. Productive inventory, as measured by dollar value, will not exceed N dollars during N months.

51. The value set on obsolete or salvage materials will not be less than N percent of its original value.

52. Inventory on materials and supplies is handled by EDP, determined by formula and reordered through "check points." Computer printouts are run on items older than N months.

53. Inventory in use is moved within N minutes from station to station.

54. Each manager and his or her department head will review the performance of the unit under the manager's control within N days of the end of each report period. Managers will be reviewed openly on their performance against plan.

55. Reports of performance against plan are generated daily and in the hands of managers within N hours of the end of the work shift or working day.

56. The plant manager will make a personal tour of the plant at least once a day.

57. Information needs of various department heads and managers are reviewed every N months and judgments of their actual needs against the costs of generating this data are made. Nonessential elements of information are eliminated.

58. Cost of machine A repairs will be reduced from N dollars to N dollars during N year.

59. One technique in work simplification will be developed for Plant A during an N-month period through weekly cost-reduction meetings between affected workers and supervisors.

60. EDP system for N departments will be installed to replace N dollars of clerical labor, with the system's leading and operational costs not to exceed N percent of the projected savings.

61. Inventory lead time will be reduced from N weeks to N weeks while maintaining standards of production.

62. A master schedule of sales will be compared to inventories at N intervals to reduce stock frequency rates to N percentages during N year.

63. Material-handling costs will be reduced to N percent of manufactured costs by new process layouts in the X plant by N year.

64. A vendor-rating system will be completed by N date to establish reliability, price and delivery for all vendors to achieve competitive bidding for materials at or below an index achieved for last period.

65. Stock rejects of product X items will be reduced by N date to N percent of all items in plant A during N year.

66. Heat losses at N percent or less of all heat transferred will be achieved when moving Product N from system X to system Y.

67. Shipping costs will not exceed N dollars per unit of Product N from shipping point A to shipping point B.

68. All subordinates will be met at their work stations briefly once a day to ascertain status of work. Once every N days the manager will hold a work appraisal meeting personally in his office with each subordinate and openly review work performance.

69. While completing Project A, Plant B will maintain overtime hours at the rate of no more than N percent of scheduled hours.

70. Customer complaints because of quality control or incorrectly shipped items will not exceed N percent of all items shipped per year.

71. Orders are shipped according to customer specifications when shipping is paid for by the customer. Otherwise, they will be shipped by the least costly but effective method. In no instance will shipping time between plant and receipt by customer exceed N days.

Production Management Performance Monitors

72. Manpower productivity and performance

73. Value analysis

74. Manufacturing costs

75. Costs per unit

76. Purchasing costs

77. Variances in costs

78. Lead time for production

79. Production backlogs

80. Costs of overtime

81. Standard cost vs. actual

82. Shipping costs

83. Percentage of projects completed vs. planning

84. Equipment obsolescence and depreciation trends

85. Inventory levels compared with sales levels

86. Back order rates and categories

87. Inventory levels compared with back order levels

88. Deadlines achieved in terms of percentages

89. Performance variance as a percentage compared with budgets

90. Percentage of labor capacity's utilization

91. Comparison between machine hours per item and total process items

92. Correlation of output and input between equipment use and labor capacity

93. Percentage of company production compared with work which is farmed out

94. The frequency rate for rescheduling production

95. Work behind schedule aging

96. Ratio of productive output per unit of labor input

97. The ratio of new personnel hired to experienced production workers

98. Ratio of assets to inventory

99. Turnover of inventory

100. Rework percentages and trends

101. Ratio of net sales to inventory

102. Percentage of available floor space actually used

103. Percentage of capital equipment actually used

104. Equipment down-time percent vs. age and profile

105. Percentage of material handling compared to unit cost

106. Scrap, reject or waste percentages and trends

107. Order error percentages

108. Completion rates measured by task-time

109. Correction ratios for defects

110. Scrap and waste percentages and trends

111. Setup preparation time percentages

112. Safety stock depreciation frequencies

113. Ratios of demand time to supply time

114. Levels for minimum lead time reordering

115. Queue ratios

116. Machine capacity and actual utilization

117. Dollars and units of output

118. Dollars and units of shipments

119. Production occupancy of available footage

120. Units and dollars of waste, scrap or rejects

121. Breakdown reports

122. Consumption of utilities

123. Production equipment
- condition
- upkeep costs
- age

124. Usage of shop supplies and nondurable tool consumption

125. Material yields compared with:
- raw material consumption
- material cost
- shrinkage (if applicable)
- direct labor
- manufacturing cycle timing

126. Productivity:
- net output per worker hour
- net output per unit of labor and tangible capital
- net output per unit of weighted tangible capital

127. Percentage of employees on incentives

128. Average earnings as percentage of base rate

129. Number of engineering personnel to number of factory workers

130. Number of production and inventory control personnel in relationship to total plant employment

131. Inventory performance measurements:
- dollars invested in inventory
- turnover rate of inventory
- inventory declared surplus or obsolete
- costs of holding inventories
- actual material costs vs. estimated material costs
- levels of backup stock

• percentage of shortages of inventory
• inventory items of which no distribution was made, as a percentage
• actual levels of inventories compared with planned levels

132. Number of employees

133. Employees on regular wages

134. Employees on incentive plans

135. Employees on standards

136. Employee overtime in man-hours

137. Man-hours of each cost center

138. Factory engineering: man-hours; dollars

139. Materials handling: man-hours; dollars

140. Factory warehousing and shipping expenses

141. Clerical: man-hours; dollars

142. Quality control and inspection: man-hours; dollars.

143. Tool and fixture making: man-hours; dollars

144. Setup time: man-hours; dollars

145. Maintenance and repair: man-hours; dollars

146. Housekeeping and sanitation: man-hours; dollars

147. Production planning establishes workload of each machine and operator with sufficient lead time so that production can adequately forecast and schedule manpower and machine priorities.

148. Production standards include machine speeds and optimum rates of production. The best workers are scheduled to get the most challenging jobs on the best machines.

149. The current status of any order can be readily determined in minutes.

150. Coordination between sales and production allows sales forecasts to be prepared in sufficient detail so that these may be readily translated into specific production planning.

151. Production schedules are widely communicated among persons who will be responsibile for them and are also posted and otherwise prominently displayed.

152. Both production and production control double-check the accuracy of records.

153. Customers and others are given a means to communicate their ideas to make production operations more effective, suitable or profitable.

154. Materials availability is always double-checked before production begins so that there are no shortages which will slow down or curtail the production run.

155. The actual cost of the quality control department has been checked within N months and represents no more than N percent of production costs.

156. All major jobs and operations have time standards, machine speeds, work standards, and other data established prior to production runs.

157. Continuous reviews, occurring every N months, analyze methods and operations as well as standards for their pertinence, productivity and effectiveness. Those production methods or standards not meeting the criteria of this review are revised or withdrawn and replaced by new thinking.

158. Actual production is compared with planned production daily and deviations are analyzed so that future production will conform with planning.

159. Time recording data is double-checked for accuracy and reliability.

160. Delays of production are communicated, along with estimated timetables, to all affected departments.

161. All applicable company departments are considered when make-or-buy decisions are encountered. Costs are analyzed and known before contracts are let.

162. Scrap items are recorded and logged. This record is used as a measure of worker effectiveness as well as a method of reducing cost.

163. Equipment performance is inspected at intervals after its installation to be certain it functions up to design and designated standards.

164. Idle-time reports are prepared for machines and workers to be analyzed for causes of idleness and to boost productivity.

165. Delays or interruptions causing idle time are checked and causes are systematically eliminated.

166. Delays or interruptions are compared against planning so that production schedules are consistent with realistic expectations.

167. Steps in all operations are analyzed to determine if certain steps can be modified or eliminated so the process may be simplified and made more efficient.

168. Operations are analyzed to determine which components or production steps can be divided and later combined more effectively with other operations.

169. Small parts used in quantity are weighed rather than individually counted.

170. Materials handling is analyzed for cost reductions through the use of bulk or other specialized methods including pallets, hoists, forklift trucks, conveyors, skids, etc.

171. Repetitive functions which call for little human judgment are analyzed from the point of view of automating the job.

172. New and technically advanced machinery and equipment are analyzed for possible purchase based on economic justification and practicality.

173. Plant work areas are analyzed every N months for needs of modernization and upgrading, including work arrangements, new lighting, painting in bright colors, industrial carpeting, etc.

174. Time and motion studies have been completed on manufacturing and warehousing areas so that all machinery, equipment and materials are placed for most efficient production. These studies have been performed by outside specialists and are undertaken every N months.

175. Efficiency of machines and their conformance to standards are checked every N months.

176. Warehousing is efficient and well laid out, vertically as well as horizontally, with vertical storage and shelving area used the height of the area and serviced by forklift trucks.

177. Inventory and production records are checked for actual use of materials to determine that all materials are accounted for.

178. Inventory areas are separate from production areas, and systems are in effect to discourage pilferage or waste.

179. Shipping as well as receiving areas are under control systems to safeguard materials from pilferage. No strangers or unauthorized persons are allowed to spend time in these areas without proper supervision, nor is any employee allowed to take materials without proper control authorizations. Valuable portable items are fenced off and under lock and key.

180. Systems are in effect so that all incoming and departing materials are checked against itemized lists.

181. Machines or operations which are critical in the productive cycle have a backup operator trained and ready to take over so that output is not stopped in the event of operator illness or accident.

182. The ratio of workers to supervisors is such that output is high but supervisors can still take care of their work duties.

183. Supervisors are trained to provide job direction to those who need it and have enough time to perform this important function.

184. Systematic training provides attitudes, knowledge and skills in porblem solving and cost controlling.

185. There is a "career pathing" program in effect so that employees who have the necessary qualifications and proper motivation can advance in the company.

186. "Job posting" occurs throughout the plant so that all employees have knowledge of every opening in the company and have an opportunity to better themselves.

187. Standards exist and are well understood for the ranking of every employee in relationship to his or her work. Rewards are given only for accomplishments and results, not for effort, for personality traits, or for activities.

188. Extensive programmed training involving written material and testing is given every employee prior to his or her being held accountable for any job. Employees are thus well trained for the job they are about to perform.

189. Workers and supervisors alike cooperate in "task team" efforts to solve production and cost problems.

190. Positions in supervisory or managerial posts opening up through retirement are identified N years in advance, and suitable replacements are identified and trained.

191. Turnover ratios of workers or supervisors in any department do not exceed the ratio in other departments or for the industry as a whole.

192. Analysis has been made of the suitability and possible productivity gains of such scheduling procedures for workers as "flex time," in which workers schedule their own working hours about a core time in cooperation with their work unit and other departments while meeting standards and departmental goals.

193. Analysis has been made of the "work team" approach or similar approaches whereby teams of workers handle one process from start to completion while still being held accountable for all production schedules and standards.

Production Management Performance Ratios

194. Production costs divided by the sales value of the production

195. Production contribution divided by production assets

196. Direct materials cost divided by the sales value of production

197. Production overhead divided by sales value of production

198. Raw material stock divided by average daily purchases

199. Finished goods stock divided by the average daily value of production completed

200. Work in progress divided by the average daily value of issues to production and the products completed

201. Value of factory plant divided by sales value of production

202. Sales value of production divided by the area of the factory plant

203. Value of plant divided by the sales value of production

204. Manufacturing plant at depreciated value divided by the plant at an undepreciated value

205. Sales value of production divided by the area of the factory plant

206. Direct labor cost divided by the sales value of production

207. Direct labor cost divided by hours worked

208. Standard hours of productive work divided by total attendance hours

209. Sales value of production divided by standard hours of productive work

210. Standard hours of productive work divided by total standard hours produced

211. Total standard hours produced divided by working time

212. Overtime hours divided by total hours

213. Overtime premium hours divided by overtime hours

214. Machine operating costs divided by the sales value of production

215. Machine fixed operating costs divided by maximum output

216. Machine variable operating costs divided by actual output

217. Actual output divided by maximum output

218. Sales value of production divided by actual output

219. Employee's basic wages divided by maximum output

220. Supervisor's basic wages divided by maximum ouput

221. Bonus output divided by actual output

222. Overtime payment divided by actual output

223. Maintenance divided by actual output

Production Management: Symptoms And Treatments

Symptom	*Treatment*
224. Low efficiency rate, excesses of essentially nonproductive work or "lost time"	Plan the work well ahead of time; schedule workers as soon as possible at each shift's beginning; transfer workers from one job to another immediately after completion of work of after machinery difficulties; keep a high level of maintenance on machinery to prevent breakdowns, and when they occur, have a system of immediate steps operative to commence repairs; develop accountability standards for each worker along with goals and objectives for each job.
225. Low machine productivity	Establish planning to set a rate of production for each job; set accountability standards for each job; be certain all machines are well maintained and ready to go, and the best workers get the best machines.

226. Low rate of worker productivity

Establish accountability of worker for specific results to be performed; set job standards; train workers in most effective methods of obtaining results; keep records of these results and keep workers informed and rewarded for special efforts; plan for a minimum amount of manpower for each job consistent with safety and other standards.

227. Not enough output because of lack of hours worked or worker shortages

Plan for higher machine and worker utilization; work as much overtime as is effective and necessary; seek and train additional workers to supplement current crews.

228. Excessive idle time on machines

Use planning and control for larger work batches or more consistent work scheduling so that as many machines as possible are fully manned at each shift's beginning; organize work flow; set job standards; establish worker accountability for results on machine, alert maintenance for repairs and adjustments for as little "down" time as possible.

229. Material quality uneven or poorer than required standards; yield from material less than desired

Keep records of purchasing's standards for vendors and check raw materials against these; inform applicable persons of significant deviations for possible actions; keep checking material systematically and frequently; be certain that process standards are strictly carried out.

230. Processing is not up to desired standards	Check the work to be certain that the workers involved are knowledgeable in processing methods and standards and correctly use them; plan ahead on how to use the material for best processing, including such details as how to cut lengths; arrange for checks often of the work with attention to factors such as finish and dimensions.

Production Management: Performance Standards

231. Production management understands and applies financial measurements focusing on return on investment and return on assets calculations as involved in production's purchasing decision, acquisition of facilities and equipment, inventory materials stocking, make-or-buy decisions, as well as production of the product line so that emphasis may be given to those products which will present the better return on the assets needed to manufacture them.

232. Standards of performance and objectives are expressed partly in terms of return on investment, return on asset calculations, as well as other ratios which quantify production management's achievement of results.

233. Objectives for each job are set and are the focal point for measurements.

234. A policy of "no surprises" is in effect whereby a problem which can be anticipated is communicated in advance for proper handling or decision making.

235. Production management has established policies for recurring decision-making situations which are repetitive and which require consistency.

236. All production policies are known to all who will make decisions.

237. Participative management policies are used to shape decisions in applicable matters.

238. Production management integrates and controls the resources provided to achieve objectives and the standards of performance required by the company.

239. Production management makes economical use of labor, equipment and materials to manufacture the company's products in the quality and quantity required to meet the company's sales commitments.

240. Production management concerns itself with all facets of production policy, production organization, human resource development, commitments and responsibilities, standards of performance, accountability, facilities and equipment and relationships within the organization as well as relationships with major customers, suppliers and the community itself in which the production plant is a "good neighbor."

241. Company policies are set for inventory levels as well as the record keeping of inventory. Determinations are made for timing, for raw materials, in-process stock, supplies and materials as well as finished stock. Part of the policies also determine standards for categorizing salvage or waste stock as well as how to sell these to reclaim part of costs.

242. Studies are made of competitors to maintain a competitive production stance.

243. Variances in policies are made in writing within N hours after action is taken. No more than N percent of decisions a year will be at variance with company policies.

244. All procedure policies have a "Sunset Clause" in them whereby they automatically lapse after N years unless specifically renewed.

245. An information system has been set up to supply all facts needed for sound production operations as well as for forecasting and planning.

246. Production management has compiled a specific management procedure manual and copies have been distributed to those who will use them. They cover such matters as purchasing determinations, inventory control, production control and scheduling, materials handling, maintenance, receiving and shipping, packaging, quality control, manufacturing specifications and processes, design specifications, product testing and inspection procedures, value engineering, capital expenditures determinations and justifications, machinery and equipment use and standards, make-or-buy decisions, measured work, accountability statements, safety requirements, manpower use, manufacturing audits and measurements, and other procedures.

247. Production management is concerned with the company's good standing in the community of which it is a part. Management is encouraged to take part in community activities and organizations. Each manager is required to belong to at least one community or civic organization which has as its goal the betterment of the community or the business climate.

248. Production management provides community or business leadership by holding office in civic or business organizations.

249. Each plant receives at least N column inches of space in the newspapers representing its community with at least N percent of these published stories having an overall favorable viewpoint to the company or reporting "objectively" of the company's actions or changes.

250. Top production management schedules at least one lunch period per month with top management of another department with the purpose of exchanging contacts and information. Each meeting is followed by an informal written report sharing needed information with departmental teams.

251. A "master file" is kept of all pertinent inputs to policy matters, including requests for variations. When X requests for variations on policy are received, the policy itself is reviewed for revision.

252. Each policy is reviewed no less than once every two years.

14

HOW TO MEASURE MANUFACTURING, INDUSTRIAL ENGINEERING MANAGEMENT PERFORMANCE

Background Data for Management

1. Has your plant's productivity been measured in the past year? The past three years?

2. Is it increasing or decreasing? Is it decreasing or increasing faster than national norms for the industry in which you compete?

3. Have internal performance measures been established for each worker? Each department? Each machine or operation?

4. How much cost reduction has actually been accomplished through specific programming this year as compared with last?

5. Are new machines considered only if the estimated cost savings represents a return of at least X percent on the investment? What is the *actual* return on investment of the latest machine purchased last year?

6. Is a system now in effect for making quantifiable analyses of machinery and equipment utilization using factors such as service costs, service life, maintenance, depreciation and other factors?

7. Have standards been established so that all products are manufactured for X percent less cost than the contracted purchase price? If any products are reaching the point where they are marginal in profitability to produce, what steps are being taken?

8. Is EDP extensively used by operational engineering? Does management routinely receive printouts of analyses?

9. Does the cost of operational engineering information gathering and analysis stay within X percent of its estimated value to the company? Do some studies far exceed any practical value?

10. Are studies, recommendations and other data based on priorities established by top management?

11. Does the department introduce at least X number of improvements in work methods annually resulting in a projected amount of N dollars of savings?

Operational Engineering Management Job Elements

12. Review plans of operating departments to determine what service or support each will require.

13. Review departmental profit improvement opportunities.

14. Set objectives.

15. Set plans for reaching objectives.

Operational Engineering Management Objectives

16. Complete construction of N, have operational by N date within capital budget of N dollars and expense budget of N dollars.

17. Re-engineer X line in X department by N date within expense budget of N dollars to achieve N percent increase in productivity.

18. Present feasibility study of acquiring X equipment by N date.

19. Conduct a long-range facility and equipment plan for corporate growth for the next fifteen years in each of the N product lines.

20. Develop by N date a standards manual for each operation which details the time and the cost for each manufacturing process.

21. Develop standards for equipment based on probable hours of use and value added to the product over N years of use.

22. Develop standards for return on investment of any new equipment.

23. Reduce material costs per unit N percent during the next N months.

24. Effect cost savings of N percent on each product during the next year through improved efficiencies in manufacturing.

25. Develop engineered cost data for N percent of the product manufacturing operations.

26. Improve the manufacturing process and production facilities to upgrade production an average of N percent.

27. Conduct an audit every N months of standard cost data including a specific audit of variances of standard against actual when variances are noted.

28. Audit the performance of each production unit or plant to achieve N percentage of cost reduction during N date.

29. Decrease manufacturing costs for products X, Y, and Z by N percent during fiscal N year.

30. Decrease scrap costs so that they do not exceed N percent of the total cost of goods manufactured.

31. Produce a value engineering study of Products A and B within the next N months.

32. Analyze and recommend each N months specific methods and equipment which will impact an N percent cost reduction when employed.

33. Complete a machine and equipment standardization program by N date.

34. Publish an operational engineering bulletin reporting monthly on the results of operations research and results which affect company production.

How to Monitor Operations Engineering Management Performance Aginst Objectives:

35. Policy has been set so that continuous variations from pre-established operations standards will be corrected within hours after first detected.

36. Project design decisions, material selections, and equipment purch-ases are not judged totally on first cost considerations but on the basis of total costs over an extended period and on total profitability.

37. Reviews and analyses of operations occur every N days with the objective of enhancing efficiency, economy and operational safety.

38. Continuing cost reduction, production enhancement and safety programs are in effect for all manufacturing units and related departments.

39. Operational engineering develops cost estimates for all new or changed products as well as develops the processes and selects equipment.

40. Requests for changes in manufacturing are reviewed by operational engineering management within N hours after their receipt and formal com-munications emanate from the department.

41. Operational engineering researches proposed methods or techniques or new equipment on a priority system set by top management. Reports based on this research are expected on a specified date.

42. New techniques are conducted in test lots and the results on suitabil ity of the technique for use in the plant is made within N weeks.

43. Operational engineering management decisions ensure that products are produced at the lowest possible cost consistent with the predetermined company standards of quality. Standards exist for each product and are widely communicated.

44. Operational engineering management makes timely recommenda-tions on methods to reduce operating costs and to increase efficiencies while maintaining company standards.

45. At least N new techniques, processes or methods to enhance productivity are proposed each year.

46. Daily reports are analyzed daily to identify areas where job performance, tools, standards or other production elements are unsatisfactory.

47. Special analyses and efforts are undertaken for process improvement, cost reduction, plant layout efficiency, equipment standards or work flow when unsatisfactory results are obtained. Recommendations for improvements will be forthcoming within N days and each recommendation will detail the estimated costs savings involved.

48. Costs of a product are estimated realistically and these costs are maintained or lowered as production increases so that prices set will yield an N return on sales as well as N percentage of the company's investment in the plant.

49. Operational engineering initiates repair, work or change orders to designate design changes, repairs, process changes and related efforts for tools, fixtures and other items in the plant.

50. Operational engineering analyzes all modified or new products to determine design changes which could reduce costs, improve quality or enhance productivity.

51. Design changes, machine or process equipment modifications or changes in plant layout or other changes over N dollars in outlay are subject to operational engineering review and approval.

52. Operational engineering considers factors of equipment standardization and parts interchangeability when machine or plant modifications are contemplated.

53. Operational engineering management works closely with purchasing to standardize parts and equipment.

54. Purchases which do not meet standards are handled by established procedures so that problem solving will be expedited and future problems such as substandard tools, different-than-standard machinery and odd-size fixtures will be eliminated.

55. Processing standards exist for all products and are in the hands of the workers who are held accountable for meeting them.

56. Operational engineering recommends processes or techniques to be used for each new product. The department continues its follow-up on recommendations by restudy of the process every N months.

57. Each month the department restudies the existing manufacturing process on at least one product component.

58. Operating units have recommendations as to the most effective and productive methods for doing tasks.

59. Standard company data are used to establish direct and indirect labor time standards.

60. Audits of direct and indirect labor standards are conducted every N months to determine consistency and accuracy.

61. Operational engineering studies replace "historic" cost data for N percent of all manufacturing operations each month.

62. A time reporting system for the use of operational engineering personnel has been developed to determine what time is spent on which project.

63. Production operations' records are surveyed every N months to determine productive hours from machines and tools, along with the down time for unscheduled and scheduled repairs as well as maintenance.

64. An updated standards manual is published which establishes standards for materials, manufacturing processes and equipment.

65. An organizational chart of the department shows current functions and responsibilities.

66. Training priorities and responsibilities are established so that each new engineer in the department receives at least N hours of productive training in his or her first three months of employment.

67. Standards and objectives are set and understood by each department member. Rewards are tied to the accomplishment of specific results. Special bonuses are offered for extraordinary cost savings or productivity enhancement based on individual initiative and tied to a percentage of the actual results accrued.

68. Management exists "in depth" for any position with successors identified and being groomed for promotion.

69. Close contacts are maintained with informational inputs including industry leaders, universities and colleges, scientific researchers as well as equipment manufacturers so that new equipment and processes which will increase profitability and cut costs are known and examined ahead of competition.

70. Material rejected initially on the production line is routinely inspected and N percent is recycled for future sale.

71. Clear standards exist and are understood as to what constitutes waste or scrap material.

72. Tolerances, finishes and related decisions are reviewed each month so that changes which will reduce costs, improve quality or expedite production can be introduced promptly.

73. New sources for material are continuously sought to improve quality, cut costs or enhance production. Alternate sources of supply, as well as alternate materials, are known and can be brought to bear as needed.

74. Systematic research compares relative qualities and costs of different methods of manufacture, machinery and materials. This research is ongoing and reported.

75. Standards of quality and value are on file with manufacturers and vendors. These are encouraged to come forth with specific recommendations for cost cutting, productivity enhancements or quality improvements.

76. Routine analyses are made on materials and replacement items so that substitutions favorable to operations can be made.

77. Patents are routinely applied for to protect company innovations.

78. Operations engineering receives as routine procedure information on all applicable new items or tools of advanced or special design or nature for possible testing to replace or to upgrade existing tools or items.

79. Cost justifications for new equipment involve estimated hours of use and value added to the product for at least N years of use as well as return on investment.

80. Equipment which is costly to use, suffers excessive repairs or down time, is not used proportionately with other equipment, is obsolete or is no longer well suited to its end use is routinely identified and recommended for replacement.

81. No equipment or machine is proposed unless the return to be realized after taxes is at least N percent.

82. Records are maintained on the status of all equipment and machinery, including the categorizing of active, inactive and surplus items. Disposal of obsolete equipment is completed in the most profitable and expeditious way possible.

83. Operating engineering makes replacement analyses on equipment utilizing such factors as space costs, depreciation, service life, productivity, efficiency, energy requirements, maintenance, service costs, or estimated down time. Initial cost alone is not the crucial determination.

84. No more than N hours of work time may be lost per year due to replacement of existing equipment parts, the installation of new equipment, or the relocation of equipment.

85. Surplus inventories are maintained and information communicated so that equipment declared surplus by one plant may be utilized by another.

86. Revised production methods, use of new materials, or changes in design are analyzed in terms of cost and profitability by operational engineering before decisions are reached.

87. Results of operational engineering are described in an annual report. The report deals with achievements, not activities, and itemizes annual savings gained, productivity enhancements or other matters dealt with quantitatively. It also presents projects under way, and the reasoning behind these projects, as well as deals with future plans.

88. Cost estimates deal with total costs including labor, material, tooling, equipment, materials handling and other related items.

89. Actual manufacturing costs for new products are within plus or minus N percent of operational engineering's estimated costs.

90. Products will be manufactured when current costs are N percent less than contracted purchase price.

91. Make-or-buy considerations for new products or existing products weigh total inputs including labor, routing sequences and operation requirements.

92. Make-or-buy decisions are calculated whenever utilization of plant capacity reaches N percent.

93. Dollar value of inventory of plant tools, fixtures and jigs will not exceed N percent of the dollar value of the manufacturing value to be added for N months.

94. Costs of in-plant production of such items as tools, dies, jigs, etc. are compared with costs to buy them outside.

95. The cost of operational engineering analysis and information will not exceed N percent of its estimated value.

96. New work methods and equipment are first calculated through operational engineering.

97. The most productive methods for plant operations have been identified in key areas and all applicable workers have been instructed in the methodology to be used.

98. Standards for direct and indirect work exist and are used for incentive programs as well as for work measurement.

99. Operational engineering is responsible for developing at least N new improvements in work methods or production each year which will produce savings of at least N dollars.

100. Operational engineering continues work simplification programming to improve productivity and to cut costs.

101. Standard practice procedures have been developed and cover at least N percent of all plant repetitive operations.

102. Each production operation is restudied at least every N months to determine areas to improve operations and to enhance productivity.

15

HOW TO MEASURE MATERIALS HANDLING MANAGEMENT PERFORMANCE

Background Data for Management

1. When was the last materials handling flow study made of your plant? Is it more than two years old?

2. What percent of production time is lost because of material, parts or equipment handling or transportation problems? How many pretax dollars are lost?

3. Is your warehouse operation based on engineered studies and data—or did it "just grow" like Topsy?

4. How many errors in shipping do audits point up? How much in damages? Demurrage? Of your total shipping bill, how much is due to "error?"

5. Is the warehouse cost efficient? That is, does it meet standards of layout so that material is quickly located and easily moved, with the material used most the most accessible?

6. What is the cost per ton-mile? Is it increasing greatly?

7. Are goods or materials on the average moved to the next work station or to finished goods storage within N minutes?

8. What percentage of customer complaints can be attributed to shipping or materials handling?

9. What are your materials handling maintenance charges per month? Per year? Is this increasing or decreasing?

10. Do materials or items seem to be piled up haphazardly in certain areas? Do workers seem to be standing about idle?

Materials Handling Management Performance Objectives

11. Complete a flow analysis of materials, parts work in process, finished goods and customer orders handled from N date to N date.

12. Compile engineered standard data for N percent of all operations by N date.

13. Study in depth at least one new material handling procedure every N months with the specific objective of possibly using this procedure to eliminate a traditional bottleneck or problem within the plant.

14. Reduce lost time due to materials handling problems from N hours to N hours during N year.

15. Move work in process or inventories from one work operation to the next or to finished goods storage within N minutes after receipt of request.

16. Dispatch requisitions against general stores within N minutes.

17. On-time shipping will increase to N percent of all shipments during N year.

18. Reduce misdirected shipments from each area to N percent of all shipments during N year.

19. Reduce materials handling budget by N percent during N year through installation of new equipment and procedures.

20. Develop standards categorizing surplus or obsolete material, as well as procedures for disposing of these, so that all such material will be removed within N days after determination.

21. Reduce demurrage charges to N percent of N dollar value of materials.

22. Set up and maintain equipment so that every machine receives an inspection every N working hours and an overhaul every N miles or hours.

Materials Handling Management: Performance Measurements and Ratios

23. The ratio of material handling personnel in comparison with 100 factory employees

24. The ratio of total number of material handling moves to the total number of operations

25. Tons carried per vehicle per year

26. Costs per ton-mile per year

27. The ratio of long hauls compared with short hauls

28. Maintenance cost per unit

29. Materials handling costs as a percentage of manufacturing costs per year

30. Percentage of time lost by production due to faulty material handling

31. Percentage of total time that material handling equipment, such as forklift trucks, are actually used

32. Labor costs per ton of materials handled

33. Cost of maintenance of equipment per ton-mile

34. The ratio of less than truckload lots or less than carload lots shipped in comparison to carload or truckload lots

35. Frequency and value of lost or damaged goods per shipment

36. Ratio of customer complaints compared with shipments

37. Ratio of demurrage charges compared with total shipments

38. Percentage of warehouse floor space actually utilized

39. Ratio of materials handling time consumed compared to the total manufacturing cycle time

How to Monitor Materials Handling Management Performance Against Objectives

40. The value of products or materials stored per square foot is at least N dollars.

41. Stockrooms and warehouse have sufficient organization to fill requests for materials or supplies within N minutes.

42. Materials are arranged by priority needs, with those used most often being the most accessible. Studies have determined warehouse priorities.

43. Materials handling has sufficient staff so that there is no "bottleneck" for effective production.

44. The average stock request is filled with N minutes.

45. The ratio of stockroom requisitions per employee is not less than N percent.

46. Materials handling personnel are notified in advance of large planned changes in work or inventory.

47. Materials handling has a clear-cut line of supervision and management with responsibilities and objectives.

48. One person has the function of keeping abreast of all new materials handling methods or equipment. Detailed engineering studies provide data on new items' profitability to the company.

49. Warehouse and shipping areas are laid out according to engineering studies for utmost effectiveness. These are kept orderly and "workmanlike," with no evidence of materials piled up haphazardly or without purpose.

50. Materials are not moved more than is necessary.

51. Materials and products are contained in the most easily handled forms and in the units in which they will be shipped.

52. Aisles comprise N percent of the plant, are well lighted, and are kept free of materials so as not to interfere with traffic.

53. Production areas maintain a flow of work. There are no clutters of materials or parts to be moved along which indicate haphazard materials handling.

54. Prepackaged cartons are used to simplify counts.

55. Materials are palletized for loading or unloading with machine assistance.

56. One new item of material handling is tested each year.

57. Stockrooms are analyzed every N months and laid out according to priorities in which the fastest-moving items are concentrated closest to requisition areas to minimize travel and retrieval time and to enhance productivity.

58. Materials handling management takes the initiative in recommending new methods for materials handling, storage and warehousing.

59. Shipping and storage areas are adjacent or close by so that costly extra hauling may be eliminated.

60. All storage bins are well lighted and clearly labeled, and items are neatly stored with contents easy to see at a glance.

61. Breakage or other losses in dollars due to careless or rough handling is less than N percent of all materials.

62. Receiving reports are routinely checked against bills of lading. Both are checked in detail against the original requisitions.

63. Systems and procedures are in effect for handling deficiencies and damage to all materials, supplies and equipment.

64. Warehouse procedures control what will be stored in various areas as well as how materials are logged in and out.

65. All merchandise which should be stored uncartoned is so stored and displayed to facilitate identification and save time.

66. N percent of all incoming shipment cartons or items are examined in detail for conformance to specifications and for absence of damage.

67. A vendor is notified within N hours of company receipt of shipment if the vendor's products do not meet purchase or other requirements.

68. Inventory records are kept up to date for all products and materials in the warehouses. These records are verified every N months by actual count or measure.

69. Inventory discrepancies which are uncovered by monthly inventory verification are investigated within N hours and a report detailing corrective action taken sent within N hours.

70. Actual inventories do not vary from inventory records by more than N percent.

71. No more than N percent of warehouse space is used for inventory which is classified as obsolete or scrap.

72. Standard procedures involving bidding are used to dispose of obsolete or scrap inventory. It is sold for no less than N dollars per hundred pounds.

73. Costs of warehousing are no more than N dollars per square foot and total warehouse costs do not exceed N dollars per $100,000 of inventory valuation.

74. Standard systems of parts numbers are used.

75. Daily labor costs analysis forms have been developed and are in use.

76. Work measurement studies have been completed and wage incentive plans for materials handling workers are based on these.

77. Work studies have been conducted so that materials are available without waste motion or unnecessary effort.

78. Forklift trucks are in use in the warehouse and plant.

79. Shipments are ready for loading N percent of the time so that no time is wasted.

80. Employees have received training in packing and shipping techniques. New materials and techniques are studied. They have the latest shipping schedules, requirements and rates.

81. No more than N percent of shipments have been sent out by a more expensive transportation mode than necessary.

82. Shipping always checks several alternatives on routes and methods of shipment so that the least expensive and most desirable shipment is always made.

83. Audits show that N percent of all shipments conform to "lowest cost" policy, when applicable.

84. Customers' orders are shipped on time for the date promised on N percent of all orders.

85. The shipping department has comprehensive rate and routing guides which are up to date.

86. A vehicle is always available to make interdepartmental or interplant deliveries every N hours.

87. Audits show that no more than N dollars' worth of shipments suffered damage due to faulty packaging.

88. Dispatched travel is controlled so that no more than N percent of all vehicles are "deadheaded."

89. Investigation is immediately launched should any loss or damage claims show a pattern.

90. When shipment weights do not equal minimum carload weights, extra shipments are evaluated for a "free" ride. Savings in this manner are recorded and rewarded.

91. Freight rates are checked against shipping orders, proper receiving and shipping documents are checked against quantities received, and loss or damage claims are noted immediately.

92. Losses due to various causes, including pilferage, do not exceed N percent of inventory per month.

93. The department uses an outside freight audit agency to supplement its own services.

16

HOW TO MEASURE MAINTENANCE MANAGEMENT PERFORMANCE

Background Data for Management

1. What are your company's actual maintenance costs, including down time from emergency repair, lost work hours, etc.?

2. Are these costs increasing or decreasing?

3. Is the department essentially seen as a "working" department staffed by craftsmen? Is it an engineering-oriented department, providing a source of information and data about your company's operations?

4. Is the work of the department "charged" to other departments when work is performed for them?

5. Is any more than 10 percent of maintenance's time spent at "emergency" repairs? Do certain jobs of this category continue to recur?

6. Have work and job standards been established for maintenance employees? Is the departmental effort primarily directed by engineered data—or "historic" job activities?

7. Can maintenance respond in one hour or less to a plant emergency or urgent need?

8. Are records of machine repairs, time spent on certain jobs, amount of down time, etc., maintained in a central file? Are these data used when machine replacements are being considered or need to be economically justified?

9. How much of maintenance's work-hours are backlogged? Is this more than 10 percent?

10. Are maintenance repairs timed so that the productivity of the plant is least impeded? Or is maintenance work done at the convenience of the crew?

Performance Objectives for Maintenance Management

11. Reduce production time lost from machine breakdown from N percent to N percent of all productive hours.

12. Decrease maintenance cycle in Plant A by N percent.

13. Establish a preventive maintenance schedule through the engineered use of historic information for Machine B to reduce its down time N percent.

14. Establish maintenance prevention programming for Equipment C.

15. Establish a maintenance program to achieve optimum maintenance costs through determination of replacement from wear in relation to the replacement costs of equipment.

16. Preplan maintenance schedules from studies of machine utilization records so loss of plant productivity because of machine down time will be minimized.

17. Reduce maintenance costs in Plant A by N percent during the next twelve months while maintaining maintenance standards of performance.

18. Establish an annual record of total maintenance costs to the company, which is a composite of the costs of labor and materials, the cost of lost production through down time and the actual cost of replacing worn out equipment (the price of the new equipment minus the value of the equipment replaced).

19. Emergency repairs to production equipment will be begun within N hours after notification and will be completed according to engineered standards and within N hours of prescribed maintenance time.

20. Establish by N date a work-order system for all maintenance effort.

Ratios and Measurements for Determining Maintenance Productivity

21. Value of products produced per maintenance dollar

22. Percentage of actual time worked in relationship to hours employed

23. Maintenance costs as a percentage of costs per unit of product

24. Maintenance costs as a percentage of plant investment

25. Percentage of total operating time lost due to maintenance

26. Maintenance employee numbers compared with N production employees

27. Maintenance employees per 10,000 square feet of manufacturing area

28. Percentage of maintenance man-hours on planned work

29. Percentage of maintenance man-hours authorized for overtime

30. Percentage of maintenance man-hours spent in doing emergency work

31. Percentage of maintenance man-hours on preventive maintenance

32. Maintenance man-hours on current backlog

33. Maintenance man-hours of total backlog

Maintenance Management Ratios to Monitor Performance Toward Objectives

34. Establishment of the ratio between the desired level of maintenance and the allowable loss of productive time from breakdowns

35. Establishment of the optimum rate of replacement from wear in relation to the level of maintenance and to the replacement costs of plant and equipment

36. Establishment of the economic values for standards of product quality and for workmanship in relation to repairs and overhauls

37. Establishment of the extent of preplanning and scheduling of maintenance activities

38. Establishment of standards and estimates as a factor in maintenance control

Informational Background for Maintenance Management

39. Historic information, primarily information on the work previously done on items which required maintenance

40. Technical information, which consists of specifications for operating, maintaining and repairing equipment

41. Policy information, which is data based on experience and provided for instruction in maintenance operations

42. Organizational information, which is documentary descriptions of the functions and the responsibilities of maintenance, including the responsibilities of inter- or intradepartmental employees.

Targets for Best Cost Maintenance

Lowest cost maintenance can be achieved by

43. Properly determined maintenance levels and practices

44. Properly trained employees working with preselected tools and materials

45. Operating under properly established controls and standards

Performance Standards of Maintenance Managers

46. All maintenance work projects are detailed by written instructions based on engineered data. Equipment is neither "overmaintained" nor maintained infrequently so as to cause problems.

47. Repair work on equipment is scheduled so that the productivity of the plant is least impaired and down time is minimized.

48. Maintenance costs are not "fixed" but variable according to engineered data.

49. Schedules, standard procedures and maintenance data are followed and maintenance is completed on specified projects within N hours of scheduled time.

50. Maintenance standards reflect management's decision on the level of plant and equipment maintenance needed to minimize down time and cost while providing the desired production quality.

51. A work-order system is in effect for prioritizing work and for providing managerial control over specified jobs.

52. The quality of information available from records is high and precise. It is used as a basis for decision making on replacement policies and maintenance schedules; on preventative maintenance work as opposed to replacement; on replacement as opposed to rebuilding; and on in-house work as opposed to outside "contract" work.

53. Maintenance repairs are checked by qualified supervisors or engineers after completion. Maintenance employees work "by the book" on all repair projects, and to predetermined engineering performance standards.

54. Repair work categorized as "emergency" is begun within N minutes/hours after the occurrence.

55. A backup plan, with standby equipment, is ready in the event of a utility failure. Employees are trained in procedures and equipment so that the switchover to the backup plan will take no more than N minutes.

56. Less than 10 percent of down time due to productive equipment failure is due to maintenance reasons.

57. Emergency and high priority work constitutes less than 15 percent of the total of all maintenance man-hours.

58. At least 85 percent of all maintenance man-hours is planned and scheduled.

59. Recurring maintenance problems which may indicate an engineering failure are turned over to specialists for permanent solutions.

60. Maintenance work involving production scheduling or other departments is coordinated and planned in advance. Schedules, with completion times, are published and distributed.

61. Certain maintenance jobs are estimated for labor and materials prior to work.

62. Each job is checked for the need of maintenance repairs and for applicable procedures prior to repair. The job is covered by a job work order.

63. Maximum cost levels are set for various maintenance jobs. Any deviation calls for additional approval.

64. Maintenance works under a budget system based on productivity objectives and on estimated workloads.

65. A task team meets regularly with the objective of reviewing costs and work so that maintenance costs may be reduced and the department may become more accountable and productive.

66. Costs of providing maintenance are at least N percent lower than the cost of the same service provided by an outside firm on a contract basis.

67. Explanations of variances in costs are submitted to the maintenance manager within N hours after completion of a project.

68. Published standards of performance are used to measure actual performance for all projects undertaken by maintenance.

69. Outside contracts are let only after receipt of at least three competitive bids based on written job specifications and dates.

70. Records of costs are maintained and analyzed based on work orders issued compared with actual costs. Deviations beyond N percent are promptly investigated.

71. Maintenance has adequate plant protection systems in operation as well as effective fire-fighting equipment and organization.

72. Maintenance holds a published inventory of equipment, repair parts and tools as well as materials and supplies for which it is responsible. This inventory is continuously maintained so that spare parts, etc., are reordered at a needed point.

73. Snow removal from the parking lots and all driveways will be completed before 7 A.M. each day and additional snow plowing and removal will continue when a depth of two inches has fallen.

74. Maintenance continuously studies new methods and processes and introduces at least N new methods each twelve months.

75. A task team, specifically composed for the purpose of maintenance productivity studies, reports its recommendations every twelve months.

76. Each employee is alert to opportunities of work simplification and productivity gains while maintaining work standards. Employees are rewarded for good ideas that contribute to overall efficiency.

77. Work standards have been developed for 80 percent of all jobs and these are based on engineered data involving time study, work sampling or other methods to produce the required level of performance in a minimal amount of time.

78. Reports are issued every N days on maintenance costs, including repair, replacement and expansion of company machinery, equipment and facilities.

79. Management checks hours of employees on jobs and equipment and material used.

80. Records are maintained on hours lost on production equipment and the time lost will not exceed N hours each twelve months.

81. No production equipment or other machine will be out of service for more than N hours for lack of spare parts.

82. The ABC machine is lubricated each N hours of use and is over-hauled after N hours of use. Complete records as to hours of use, lubrication actually given and maintenance provided are on file. Included are repair costs, time down, and other pertinent data which can be used for managerial decisions.

83. Maintenance costs will not exceed N dollars each twelve months per N dollars of value added.

84. Equipment and material stored by maintenance, which has not been used in twelve months, are reported and analyzed.

85. The cost of handling work orders has been studied and is known. A rule of thumb is that the cost of the work order will not exceed N percent of the estimated cost of the job on small maintenance items, and no more than N percent for large items.

86. To aid managerial judgments on machine value and possible re-placement, repair and other total costs for individual machines are sum-marized and reported each N months.

87. Plant lubrication programs involve periodic checklists, reports and control devices so as to assure adequate maintenance. Maintenance is abreast of the best methods and types of lubricating materials and these are used to best advantage.

88. Studies show at least N instances in which maintenance operations offer opportunities for cost reclamations of N dollars.

89. Reports are written and analyzed daily to identify areas where job performance, tools, standards or other maintenance work is lagging or unsatisfactory. Changes are decided upon and scheduled for the next day's operation.

90. Engineering studies replace "historic" methods of maintenance for N percent of all maintenance operations each month.

91. Maintenance employees have recommendations as to the most ef-fective and productive methods for performing tasks.

17

HOW TO MEASURE PLANT AND FACILITIES MANAGEMENT PERFORMANCE

Background Data for Management

1. What is your exact long-range plan for your plant and facilities five years from now? Ten years? Fifteen?

2. How much of your capital investment program provides for the improvement or the replacement of your current facilities or equipment this year? In five years?

3. At what point will it be economically justifiable for you to either expand your current facilities or build an entirely new plant?

4. Do you have a task team or facilities committee which has already identified new sites and new types of equipment or studied new and more productive plant layouts?

5. How much production time was lost due to maintenance requirements or equipment breakdown last year? How much did this actually cost the company? In the last three years? Are these costs increasing?

6. Has your plant's productivity increased or decreased during the past several years? How does this compare with your competitor's rate of productivity? Your industry's?

7. Are your actual savings from your capital expenditures within 3 percent of the planned amount?

Objectives for Plant and Facilities Management

8. Develop energy conservation measures which will save N percent of actual energy costs per month beginning N date.

9. Make a decision by N date on whether to buy new equipment X for Plant A or to lease the same equipment.

10. Develop standards for economic equipment justification on whether to maintain Equipment N, which has a remaining lifespan of three years and maintenance costs of N dollars, or to purchase new Machine H at a cost of N dollars but which has N annual maintenance costs and a lifespan of twelve years.

11. Select a site for new production Plan N by N date. Develop a siting plan by N date and develop a working model based on engineered data by N date consistent with long-range planning for 1990.

12. Develop a system for Product A which will take no more than N days to bring production facilities up to N percent of capacity to meet sales increases.

13. No more than N hours of productive time will be lost each month because of maintenance or emergencies.

Performance Measurements for Plant and Facilities Management

14. Floor space data:

• total
• movement of people and materials
• structural
• service
• net productive

15. Age of facility and attendant characteristics

16. Comparative data for total costs and for square-foot costs:

Existing Plant:	Costs for Total	Costs per Square Foot
• initial construction costs		
• rearrangements or remodeling		
• maintenance		
• repairs		
• improvements		
• additions		

New Plant:

- project management
- master planning
- architectural and engineering
- consultant and other services
- construction supervision
- construction
- moving and other related costs

17. Area utilization and vacancy:

- employees
- manufacturing
- production

18. Use of facility:

- general administrative
- direct productive
- service and support functions

19. Construction costs per area/square foot

20. Maintenance costs per area/square foot

21. Book value

22. Machine capacity/machine utilization

23. Space per person

24. Area utilization

Measurements of Facilities and Equipment

25. By return on investment

26. By square footage

27. By market value

28. By production (units or dollar value)

29. By original cost

30. By reliability values

31. By acreage or lot size

32. By depreciation

33. By fuel or energy consumption

34. By maintenance cost

35. By obsolescence

36. By power cost

37. By rent expense

38. By scrap expense

39. By taxes paid or assessments

40. By throughputs; time and expense

41. By turn-in value

42. By facility size

43. By clearances

44. By cubic foot

45. By visual inspection

46. By pressure gauges

47. By audiometers

48. By clock recorders

49. By flowmeters

50. By malfunction equipment

51. By videotape or motion picture camera

52. By production counters

53. By speedometers

54. By electrical meters

55. By vibration gauges

56. By x-ray

57. By various other devices of measurement

Measurements of Products and Materials Management Effectiveness

58. Use of order points

59. Purchase requisitions

60. EDP systems

61. Invoices

62. Costs of holding inventories

63. By inventory count

64. By inventory breakage

65. By inventory turnover

66. Back orders on hand

67. By customer complaints

68. By feedback from the field sales force

69. Bills of lading

70. Deliveries

71. By manufacturing time

72. By quantity of rework

73. Statistical quality control

74. By waste or scrap produced

75. Shipments of units

76. Dollar value on products produced

77. By visual inspection

78. By measuring devices

79. By counting or weight

80. By hardness, viscosity or other property

81. By meter

82. By scale or by rule

83. By other specialized devices

Relationship of Management Objectives and Benefits

Objectives	*Benefits*
84. Determine major physical plant and facilities needs.	Management time is directed toward the most important planning issues.
85. Capital budgeting is linked to strategic facilities requirement planning by including capital budget as part of the first two years of the facilities requirements plan.	Decisions pertaining to current budgeting and spending will be governed by long-range objectives during a traditional "weak" point.
86. Make in-depth analysis and studies of existing facilities to determine their usefulness for meeting future needs, as an alternative to building a new plant.	Provides quantitative base for managerial decision making based on the most economical methods of meeting plant needs. Can determine maximum use of existing facilities, or can aid in a combination of existing low-cost and new facilities.
87. Quantify long-range planning to include new facilities acquisition.	Production needs will be forecast, as will cost of facilities and production capabilities. All these variables can then be considered in time to make decisions and specific plans to meet goals that are set.
88. Consider strategic facilities requirements prior to practical planning.	Insures that long-range needs are factored into shorter-range planning.
89. Prioritize facilities requirements.	Allows for the most needed items to be considered first for first allocation of financial resources
90. Determine geographic location of new facilities after consideration of new energy or economic factors.	Constrains location of new facilities to areas where adequate energy sources, labor and transportation capacities meet company standards.

Managerial Informational Needs and Their Source Elements

Needs	*Source*
91. Complete inventory data of major physical facilities, including:	Fixed asset management

- productivity
- cost
- age
- useful life
- condition
- product capability
- rated capacity
- functional description

92. Projected volume, new product mix, timing objectives for proposed market and products	Marketing and Product specialists
93. Cost history of facility	Fixed assets accounting
94. Analysis of existing facilities to show which facilities have the major expenses	Fixed assets management
95. Projected cost or other effects of technological change pertinent to facilities	Outside experts and source material specialists
96. Long-term economic forecasts, analysis of chief competitors' strengths and strategies, analysis of company R & D as well as plant and facilities	Marketing, R & D, and outside source material specialists
97. Data on time requirements to plan and complete certain plant facilities which are common to the industry	Fixed asset management and outside source material specialists

98. Data on facilities required to meet planned changes in market and in product

Products, marketing specialists

99. Data on future labor, energy, and transportation needs to meet requirements of planned facilities, including:

Labor: Skills, education, unemployment, literacy, demographic data about working-age population contained within commuting distance of new plant.
Transportation: Availability of surface transportation to and from a new facility
Energy: Including adequacy of all energy sources and their costs; special problems
Pollution control requirements: Including specific regulations applicable

External source material specialists, including academic, private consultants, governmental and civic

100. Management standards for risk determinations and analysis

Corporate policy and strategy

101. Determination that planned facilities meet corporate strategies and priorities

Corporate policy and strategy

102. Analysis of environmental and social impact of plant and trends

Outside source material specialists, consultants

103. Development of alternative facilities plans along with their costs and risk factors

Plant and facilities plus outside specialists

Performance Testing and Checklists for Management Planning Effectiveness

Performance Problem
104. New plant does not achieve anticipated return on

Planning Data To Be Checked:
Reexamine risk levels involved to determine if alternative types of

investment and profitability even as new and similar plants are being considered.

105. One plant continues with a large backlog of production orders while other plants in different parts of the country operate at less than capacity.

106. One plant management continues with excessive capital expenditures during the first several years of opening the facility.

107. Chief competitors take better advantage of technological changes in plants and facilities.

108. Company is held back by legal means from completing facilities construction program even as new facilities are planned elsewhere.

109. Financial difficulties within the company, such as difficulty in obtaining enough equity capital or a declining rate of corporate bonds.

110. Material writedown of fixed asset valuations of the company, such as a writedown of fixed assets of large proportions due to declaring them "obsolete."

plants or facilities can achieve desired results.

Reconsider economic factors as constraints on the geographic location of future facilities

Tie capital budgeting to facilities planning by including budget as part of the first two years of facilities requirements planning.

Analyze existing facilities to determine their potential to meet changing needs and upgrade as necessary.
Analyze environmental trends, activity and regulations for determinations on future location, size and types of plant and facilities.

Analyze the impact of facility requirements and determinations on the company's capital structure.

Analyze existing facilities to keep abreast of their usefulness to meet the company's projected future needs so that a sudden, massive writedown is not needed.

Monitoring Objectives for Plant and Facilities Management Effectiveness

111. Long-range planning has quantifiable plans for future plants and facilities fifteen years out.

112. Strategic facilities plans include all marketing, manufacturing and financial needs.

113. Strategic plans are stated in dollars and are prioritized.

114. Schedules for new plants and facilities have been drawn up along with planned conversions, retention or disposal of existing facilities and costs for all.

115. Technological developments and their costs are included in all new planning.

116. Environmental and regulatory concerns and constraints are considered before final location, size or type of facility is decided upon.

117. All new facilities plans have alternative plans considered and ranked according to their relative risks.

118. Complete inventory of existing plants and facilities along with their productivity, condition, capabilities, useful life, etc., continue every N months and are monitored to note changes and trends.

119. Capital expenditures are monitored against objectives and produce savings of N percent of the amount originally planned for.

120. Standards exist to provide an organized approach for the choice of the most useful capital equipment at the time when it will be the most productive for the company. Included are standards for analyzing return on investment and maintenance costs as well as the revenue produced.

121. Capital expenditure proposals will be reviewed by all staff or task team members within N days of distribution.

122. Planning for new plants or facilities will begin N months ahead of actual construction, and planning will include specific site selection, type of structure and equipment, the architectural and consulting team and specific cost planning.

123. Analysis of current facilities for possible expansion or remodeling is compared with new facilities, and detailed alternatives are drawn so that prior data may be measured.

124. Current data on facilities and equipment are continuously being reviewed and analyzed to determine how the plant may obtain greater productivity.

125. Each plant manager recommends programs which will increase productivity or reduce costs.

126. New equipment installation or adjustment will not be allowed to cost more than N percent of its first month's productive time.

127. Plant management will overview the installation of major new equipment and is accountable for its performing up to expected standards.

128. Planning minimizes down time due to preventive or other types of maintenance. Often machines are pulled down when not "on line" or during low cycles in the production phase.

129. Annual plans prescribe maintenance schedules and specific standards for all equipment. Requirements are for maintenance every N hours of use according to latest manufacturers' specifications.

130. Annual plans for maintenance on buildings call for painting every N years, parking lot maintenance every N months, floor resurfacing every N months, bricks and concrete work patched every N months, and so on.

131. No major item under the management of plant and facilities is without a maintenance plan and schedule.

132. Preventive maintenance is scheduled so that lost time attributable to it is minimized.

133. Plant and facilities management makes recommendations for additional investments in production facilities which will improve productivity, reduce operating costs or improve product quality.

134. Overhaul of major equipment is scheduled during the time of the annual plant shutdown.

135. Capital investment programming follows established procedures and standards so that at least N percent of the plant's facilities and equipment is replaced each year.

136. Supervisors and employees who actually perform the specified work have inputs into the standards for the work to be completed. Their advice is routinely solicited and productivity-enhancing or work-saving methods are rewarded through a special productivity bonus based on estimated annual savings.

137. Plant and facilities supervisors are trained in basics of human behavior and can utilize behavior reinforcement to help shape employee work patterns. Authoritarian or "heavy handed" supervision is being replaced by basic operating techniques of behavioral psychology.

138. "Task team" approaches by employees themselves are used in some applicable situations, and the productivity enhancement resulting from this approach is carefully monitored for other applications.

139. Outside consultants are routinely used for inputs into plant, equipment or employee productivity. Such consultants are results-oriented, have the impact for achieving specific results desired by the company, and are selected on the basis of proven "track record" of accomplishments with similar companies.

140. Employees have inputs into safety standards they work under.

141. A study has been made to determine the effectiveness of "flex time" to give employees more control over the specific hours they work and to enhance employee productivity.

142. Employee turnover does not exceed N percent of all employees annually.

143. Absenteeism does not exceed N percent of all worker-hours per week.

144. All job openings are posted so that employees have "first chance" to fill job slots. Standards for each new job are also set and communicated.

18

HOW TO MEASURE QUALITY
ASSURANCE MANAGEMENT
PERFORMANCE

Background Data for Management

1. What percent of the sales price is your quality assurance cost?

2. Can quality assurance costs be lowered by reducing the quantity of rejects?

3. Are quality assurance's efforts determined by managerial priorities and in accordance with product value and need? Or does quality assurance essentially come up with its own standards?

4. Are there quality assurance training and standards for each operator, with each operator assuming certain quality responsibilities and being held accountable for meeting them?

5. Does quality assurance work directly with customers on complaints which arise primarily because of "poor" quality? Does management receive complete and accurate reports?

6. Are standards set so that no more than N number of units or pieces are rejected by quality assurance? Or, of those units which have been manufactured, are objectives quantified so that no more than N units are returned as being of "poor" quality either by later work stations or by customers?

7. Are tests, samples, etc., run on prototypes to eliminate not only production problems but quality assurance problems as well?

8. Does quality assurance go beyond finding existing problems in quality control to help eliminate problems before they get into the mainstream of production?

Quality Assurance Management Job Responsibilities

9. Quality assurance develops tests and measurements which are applied at various stages of the manufacturing process so that products meet planned standards.

10. It collects data so that deviations from standards can be detected early, corrected and thus prevented from entering the remaining production.

11. It checks purchases so that raw materials and parts meet standards required.

12. It works with management, supervisors and workers to maintain quality assurance standards.

13. It inspects and checks finished products as well as shipped products to be certain these products will reach customers in good order.

14. It works with customers and company personnel to determine causes of problems in products in the field to analyze changes to alleviate future problems of design, of manufacture methods, of materials or assembly.

Quality Assurance Management Performance Objectives

15. Reduce quantity of rejects of Product X by N percent.

16. Reduce quality assurance expenses by N percent.

17. Reduce unit inspection by N percent by installing approved new test equipment by N date within capital budget of N dollars and expense budget of N dollars.

Quality Assurance Management Measures of Performance

18. Quality control costs in comparison with product costs

19. Number of rejects

20. Percentage of staff time actually spent inspecting

21. Number of quality control personnel per N factory employees

22. Number of items reworked to meet quality assurance standards in relation to total number of items produced

23. Quality control costs per month and year

24. Quality control costs as a percentage of sales per month

25. Quality control costs as a percentage of product warranty and field costs per month

26. Quality assurance time as a percentage of total production time per product line

27. Final-product problems due to lack of quality assurance controls

Quality Assurance Management Performance Monitors

28. Quality assurance samples at least N percent of all purchased material.

29. Written standards cover all quality assurance efforts.

30. Company products by line are tested against established standards, and the resulting information is used to produce at least one significant improvement in each product each year.

31. The quality assurance standards applied to each product are in conformance with the product's established value and need, as determined by management.

32. All activity is budgeted, and the department submits regular reports of performance against budget.

33. Quality assurance costs do not exceed N percent of a product's net sales value.

34. No more than N percent of items manufactured are returned as "poor quality" by customers.

35. The staff spends at least N percent of its time on consulting assignments and maintains time records for all its daily activities.

36. Quality control accountability is shared by each machine operator or worker.

37. Training of operators or workers in quality assurance efforts and standards continues and returns at least N percent reduction in costs of inspection and rejects.

38. Production processes are changed quickly when significant variations from tolerances and specifications become evident. Significant variations from established standards are investigated within N minutes of determination.

39. Down time in production due to quality assurance will not exceed more than N hours weekly.

40. Raw materials are systematically checked by inspection, tests and other measurements against standards so that finished goods will meet approved manufacturing standards.

41. Deviations in standards detected by quality assurance are reported in writing to appropriate management.

42. Raising the level of quality assurance standards, with an accompanying rise of product quality to reduce product failures, costs less than the total product warranty and field service costs.

43. No production operation is allowed to run "out of control" for more than N minutes.

44. Quality assurance costs do not exceed more than N percent of all product warranty and field service costs per year.

45. Quality assurance costs do not exceed N percent of sales revenue per year.

46. Quality assurance estimates its costs on all projects in which the company is submitting a bid. These estimates will be within plus or minus N percent of actual costs.

47. Quality assurance continually works to improve the quality of the product, reduce costs of existing processes, and simplify operations in the manufacturing process.

48. Systematic training of workers and emphasis on process control standards, along with continuous inspection, help to cut failure rates.

49. Quality assurance objectives are written for each product and are complete with detailed plans and procedures.

50. Detailed checklists are compiled for final inspection so that manufactured units are properly inspected prior to shipment.

51. No more than N percent of all units shipped will undergo a failure involving warranty or other claims.

52. Total costs are calculated on all warranty work and customer claims due to failure, and these total costs will not exceed N percent of all items shipped.

53. Merchandise which is declared faulty is examined in detail, and written analysis of the failure is submitted.

54. Standard time data is compiled for all quality control operations, and a monthly analysis is calculated.

55. Field reports are monitored by quality asssurance for implications in control and testing.

56. Quality assurance staff people investigate major claims of product failure directly and work with the customers involved.

57. Major customers are visited at least every N months to check company products or equipment.

58. Major company vendors are visited on-site at least every N months with the aim of improving controls and quality of material purchased.

59. Each new vendor spends time with quality assurance so that the vendor understands the quality control standards of the company, specifications required, and how products will be tested. Included is information on company procedures, with respect to handling of unsuitable vendor material.

60. Policies are in effect so that when more than N percent of all materials supplied by vendor are defective, another previously selected "standby" vendor is substituted. A clause in the company purchasing agreement allows for this change, and the clause is understood by all vendors.

61. Testing is systematic, according to professional standards, and all test equipment is calibrated according to manufacturer's standards at least once every N months.

62. Quality assurance uses its data to help rate each company production unit, machine or equipment in terms of its performance, load, speed and tolerances.

63. Capability studies are undertaken to determine whether equipment and operators will be able to maintain product standards at higher speeds for various product lines.

64. The department has input into product design and also reviews product design every N months.

65. There is a routine system for collecting and analyzing information from product inspections or actual performance so that the company product maintains its predetermined standards.

66. Quality assurance is concerned not only with product quality and reliability but with the concerns of environmental, governmental, legal and consumer groups.

19

HOW TO MEASURE THE
MANAGEMENT PERFORMANCE OF
THE TREASURER

Background Data for Management

1. Does the cash budget of your company serve as a standard or yardstick of your company's performance?

2. If so, does actual cash flow deviate significantly from budgeted flows? Are there many, and recurring, points of differences?

3. Are financial ratios used to measure the financial health of the company?

4. What percentage of your current assets are tied up in inventory?

5. What is the length of your average collection period of accounts receivable?

6. Is this increasing or decreasing? How does it compare to industry standards?

7. What is your percentage increase on equity?

8. What is your strategy to maximize the liquidity velocity of your balance sheet?

9. What steps has your organization taken to achieve a higher cash velocity? Do you use SCALDER?

10. Have you set up a standard of ratios over a period of years so that you can get a fix on whether your company's financial position is improving or declining? Are financial ratios compared with those of other companies, notably chief competitors, or industry so that you can better gauge relative profitability and potential earning power?

Target Objectives for Treasureship Management

11. Reduce accounts receivable from N days to N days by N date.

12. Examine the market for rollover credit lines to replace short-term loans to pay unanticipated expenses.

13. Reexamine credit policies of the company in the light of economic conditions to "tighten up" credit lines by N percent by N date.

14. Establish procedures to upgrade the liquidity velocity of the balance sheet by at least N percent by N date.

15. Determine and begin new measuring ratios, within the company-wide financial reporting system, which concentrates management's attention on cash productivity and increasing cash return on each investment.

Responsibilities of the Treasureship Function

(As defined by the Financial Executives Institute)

16. *Provision of Capital:* to establish and execute programs for the provision of capital required by the business, including negotiating the procurement of capital and maintaining the required financial arrangements

17. *Investor Relations:* to establish and maintain an adequate market for the company's securities and, in connection therewith, to maintain adequate liason with investment bankers, financial analysts and shareholders

18. *Short-Term Financing:* to maintain adequate sources for the company's current borrowings from commercial banks and other lending institutions

19. *Banking and Custody:* to maintain banking arrangements, to receive, have custody of, and disburse the company's monies and securities and to be responsible for the financial aspects of real estate transactions

20. *Credit and Collection:* to direct the granting of credit and the collection of accounts due the company, including the supervision of required special arrangements for financial sales, such as time payment and leasing plans

21. *Investments:* to invest the company's funds, as required, and to establish and coordinate policies for investment in pension and other similar trusts

22. *Insurance:* to provide insurance coverage as required

Treasureship Management Performance Monitors

23. Profitability

24. Number of accounts receivable

25. Cash on hand

26. Credit ratings

27. Current sales price of stock

28. Working capital

29. Rate of interest or number or amount of loans

30. Dividends

31. Earnings

32. Income

33. Average collection period

34. Sale volume comparisons

35. Inventory on hand data

36. Accounts payable

37. Audits

38. Net worth

39. Notes outstanding

40. Overhead

41. SEC statements

42. Stock issued and movement

43. Surplus

44. Accounting records and procedures

45. Balance sheet information

46. Cost accounting

47. Current liabilities

48. Depreciation expenses

49. Fixed costs

50. Fixed assets

51. Funded debt

Financial Ratios for Management Measurement of Capital Efficiency

52. Liquidity ratios (measures a company's ability to meet its maturing obligations):

- *Current ratio* *(measures short-term solvency): Divide current liabilities into current assets. A rule of thumb is that current assets should be at least twice as great as current liabilities.*

- *Quick ratio* (measures ability to pay off short-term obligations without having to sell off inventories): Deduct inventories from current assets and divide the result by current liabilities.
- *Inventory to working capital* (measures the proportion of net current assets invested in inventory): Divide working capital (current assets minus current liabilities) into inventory.

53. Leverage ratios (measures the contribution of the owners in comparison with other financing):

- *Debt to total assets* (measures a company's obligation to creditors): Divide total assets into debt.
- *Times interest earned* (measures how much earnings could decline before the company would be unable to meet interest charges): Divide earnings (before interest and taxes) by interest charges.
- *Fixed charge coverage* (number of times fixed charges are covered): Divide profit (before fixed charges) by all fixed charges (such as lease payments, interest, etc.).
- *Current liabilities to net worth* (measures the amount of fund supplied by owners as opposed to amount of current debt): Divide current liabilities by net worth.
- *Fixed assets to net worth* (measures how much ownership funds are invested in assets with relatively low turnover): Divide net worth into fixed assets.

54. Activity analysis (measures how effectively a company is using its resources):

- *Cash velocity* (measures number of times cash turns over in a year, and, thus how effectively a company makes use of its cash flow): Divide cash and cash equivalents, such as short-term negotiable securities, into yearly sales.
- *Average collection period* (measures number of days sales are tied up in receivables): Divide annual sales by 360 to calculate average daily sales. Then divide average daily sales into accounts receivable.
- *Inventory turnover* (measures number of times inventory turns over): Divide inventory into sales. (Note: calculate inventory at market price since sales are calculated at market price.)
- *Total assets turnover* (measures assets turnover): Divide yearly sales by total assets.

55. Profitability ratios (calculates a company's overall effectiveness as measured by the returns from sales and investments):

- *Productivity of assets* (measures rate of return on total resources): Divide the sum of net profits after taxes, plus interest expenses, by total assets.
- *Sales margin* (measures profitability of sales): Divide net income by sales.
- *Return on net worth* (measures productivity of owner's resources committed to the business): Net profit divided by net worth.
- *Net operating margin* (measures how much unit selling price may go

down without losses resulting on an accrued rather than a cash basis): Divide net operating profit by sales.
• *Gross operating margin* (measures how much unit selling prices may go down without incurring a loss): Divide sales into gross operating profit.

Note: Use of financial ratios for managerial control should be displayed over a period of months and years to determine comparative trends internally (how the company is doing) and externally, such as with competitors or industry-wide figures (how well the company is doing in comparison with others). Together, these figures allow for a mature judgment on the company's financial performance in terms of profitability, cash flow and overall effectiveness as well as financial health.

"Scalder" Formulas for Management Enhancement of Cash and Liquidity

56. "SCALDER" (the seven sources of corporate cash and liquidity):
+S: Sales cash (cash obtained from increases in volume of gross sales, enhanced by increased productivity or decreases in cost of goods sold and "below the line" expenses)
−C: Internal cash (provided by cost control and reduction. As the ratio of sales to costs increases, cash is generated)
−A: Asset cash (provided by asset control and reduction, both absolutely and relatively, as the turn ratio [sales/assets] increases)
+L: Leverage cash (obtained from intermediate and long-term debt financing) EXTERNAL
+D: Acquisition cash (supplied by the acquired company)
+E   Equity cash (obtained from the sale of stock) EXTERNAL
+R: Reinvestment cash (internal cash supplied by the reinvestment, for *maximum cash payback,* of all the cash generated from the six preceding sources)

57. CRE (Cash return on equity)
This ratio of cash flow/equity encapsulates management's internal operating objectives:

cash flow/sales (profit margin)
sales/equity (turnover)

or

$$\frac{S - C}{S} \quad \times \quad \frac{S}{A - L}$$

58. A combination of equity return and equity formation is defined as percentage increase of equity or PI. PI exerts a multiple impact on earnings per share and is, therefore, exceedingly potent as a concept and as a strategy of business management. It is the heart of the strategy of cash.

The role of the top manager, and his or her investment objective, is the maximum production of cash from the balance sheet. The manager's entire responsibility and sole function is to maximize the liquidity velocity of the balance sheet. High cash velocity means there is no dilution of cash productivity from idle cash, low-return temporary investments or other losses or delays in putting it to work at maximum return. Liquidity prevails when cash is circulating at maximum force, speed and return, from sources to applications and back to sources, thus increasing profits.

59. Two financial performance objectives which constantly face management:

a. to generate the highest possible after-tax cash return on equity (CRE).
b. to invest that cash at the highest possible cash return on each investment, whether internal or external

60. CPF is the cash productivity factor. While CRE tells us what happened, it does not tell what made things happen. What made things happen is CPF:

$$CPF = \frac{S}{C} \times \frac{S}{A} \times \frac{L}{A}$$

Because more favorable productivity is reflected in high ratio values, S/C, S/A and L/A are called cash contribution ratios (CCR).

61. Business enterprises exist to maximize stockholder's wealth. They are wealth-creating institutions for stockholders. Their wealth is measured pragmatically, if ruthlessly, by the cash-realizable value of their shares of stock in the company, or their market price. Business can enhance stockholder wealth only by means of a total process of cash generation, whereby both the quantity (E) and the cash productivity (CRE) of equity are maximized.

Three sources of cash productivity:

a. S/C × S/A   : Internal cash productivity
b. L/A (R)   : Cash return on equity
c. ECO × ECA: PI

62. A cash productivity plan company-wide is expressed:

$$CRE = \frac{S}{C} \times \frac{S}{.\ A} \times \frac{L}{A} \quad (R)$$

63. CCR (Cash contribution ratios)

S/C and S/A ratios can be applied to each supervisor's or manager's work. This person, then, is personally responsible for this measurement. For example, the sales manager is responsible for the ratio of sales to departmental costs, sales to inventories, etc. (see individual chapters for other ratios). The same company-wide sales volume is the numerator of all CCRs because all functions and employees contribute to sales. So everyone's measurable contribution to cash productivity and CRE is that person's cost and asset denominators.

The company's growth, defined by CRE, is determined by the sum of all CCR's of the company at every level. If a person's CCR's are rising, he or she is measured as contributing to CRE; if declining he or she is measured as detracting from CRE.

64. Managerial strategy is to increase the external volume of sales to customers (S) and to increase the internal cash productivity of existing dollar volumes (Sc).

Financial Cost Controls to Enhance Corporate Liquidity

65. Collection—a simple, flexible and inexpensive cost accounting system must pinpoint product unit costs in meticulous detail, promptly and accurately. This is called "pinpoint costing."

66. Classification—costs must be organized and classified into categories as to origin and cause, location, behavioral type and the person responsible. Costs so classified can be analyzed creatively and imaginatively.

67. Comparison— costs are compared with predetermined engineered standards and budget allowances that reflect attainable good performance. Unless there is a standard to be compared with, cost collection is meaningless.

68. Communication—variances in costs are communicated promptly to the person who is cost responsible. Every cost is the responsibility of one person, who has charge of the cost and who can control the cost.

69. Changes— the person who is unitarily responsible for the cost variance changes the ongoing costing back to the standard required in an organized and controlled manner

70. Cost consciousness—all managers and supervisors are conscious of costing needs, standards and savings possibilities. Cost cash ($-C$) is seen as cash dollars, or savings opportunities, masquerading as costs. Costs everywhere are seen as cash possibilities.

71. Cost creativity—each person initiating cash-generating cost reduction proposals and projects searches imaginatively for cost-reducing improvements. All persons in the company are involved. Cost creativity is the link between cost control and cost reduction, taking the company from mechanical controls of costs against standards to intellectual and emotional involvement of each person who seeks imaginatively to better the standards.

Management Check List by "SCALDER" Sources to Determine Potential of Possible Acquisition Companies

72. Sales ($+S$ and $+Sc$)—external cash availability is evidenced by abnormally low ratios of sales/costs and sales/assets. These ratios provide attractive cash-generating opportunities for the buildup of the sales volume. Internal sales cash availability means the company's net sales cash (Sc) or sales less variable costs ($S-VC$) is well below the industry norm and provides improvement opportunities.

73. Cost ($-C$) — an abnormally small profit margin of an acquisition candidate presents sizable cash-generating opportunities from cost control and cost reductions.

74. Asset cash availability ($-A$)—very low ratios of sales/assets are symptomatic of excessive assets. Here there is substantial room for improvements including inventory turnover, receivable collections, and fixed asset utilization. These assets can be major sources of cash to new owners following acquisition. Asset cash availability is simply the denominator of sales/assets. Ratios will be increased and cash generated either by an increase in sales, by a reduction of costs, or reduction of assets in relation to sales.

75. Leverage cash availability (+L)—the company to be acquired has no funded debt, low current liabilities, and heavy actual or potential depreciation cash flow to support large borrowings at favorable rates and terms.

76. Acquisition, or developmental cash availability (+D or ECA) — the company is or could soon be placed in a position of strength to make developmental acquisitions that have high liquidity and corporate developmental potentials (as opposed to nondevelopmental acqusitions that are mere paper-swapping transactions). An equity-creating acquisition can take place because earnings and current share prices, not equity, invariably determine a company's acquisition price. Purchase price is thus below the company's equity.

77. Equity cash availability (+E or ECO)—there is currently, or could easily be developed, a receptive market for a sizable public offering of the company's stock at prices substantially above equity per share.

78. Reinvestment cash availability (+R)—capital spending programs have long been neglected. Small amounts of reinvestment cash, applied to projects almost anywhere in the business, produce abnormally high cash returns. This is the payback-generating "funnel" into which is poured all the cash produced from the acquired company's six sources of liquidity, to maximize its CRE.

79. BC (Best competitor's) Cash availability Standard.
This represents the amount of cash a company can generate from sales volume (+S), cost reduction (−C) and asset reduction (−A) if it were as efficient as the average best competitor. This ratio can be determined by comparing the company S/C and S/A ratios in every part of the business with the corresponding ratios of the most profitable companies in the industry (the BC's).

80. The 80/20 Rule
Not only is the 80/20 rule one for which objectives are set, but they represent objective-setting on those high-impact areas where maximum results may be achieved. Thus a manager can concentrate on the 20 percent of all possible CSA project that will produce 80 percent of the cash-productivity results. Or, on the 20 percent of the possible cost-reduction projects that will produce 80 percent of the cost-reduction cash. Or, the 20 percent of the sales developmental project that will produce 80 percent of the sales cash.

81. Statement of Liquidity Velocity.

A working tool of management, the liquidity velocity statement describes the sources and applications of cash, and analyzes the impact that each balance sheet item will have on cash production. It is the conclusive analytical weapon in a manager's strategy of cash liquidity. In it, the balance sheet line of demarcation, separating cause and effect, is raised to the point separating cash from everything else. It thus reflects changes in working capital velocity plus changes in current assets (except cash) and current debt. The statement not only describes the liquidity environment, but directs management to the proper areas of qualitative inquiry so that high working capital velocity may generate a high rate of profits and growth.

20

HOW TO MEASURE
CONTROLLERSHIP MANAGEMENT
PERFORMANCE

Background Data for Management

1. What is the average "age" of your accounts receivable? Has this age been increasing?

2. Have your inventory levels been going up and your cash levels down?

3. Have overall costs been escalating?

4. Are your financial operating reports prepared in such a manner that *variances* are highlighted—or hidden?

5. Are all major expenses and costs under strict budget control?

6. Do your financial controls include a variable budget?

7. Is return on investment measured at regular intervals by product or by project?

8. Does the company calculate and analyze its break-even point by product line or project?

9. Are systematic methods being employed to reduce costs?

Controllership Functions and Overall Objectives

(As defined by the Financial Executives Institute)

10. *Planning for Control:* To establish, coordinate, and administer, as an integral part of management, an adequate plan for the control of operations. Such a plan would provide, to the extent required in the business, profit planning; programs for capital investing and for financing, sales forecasts, expense budgets and cost standards, together with the necessary procedures to effectuate the plan.

11. *Reporting and Interpreting:* To compare performance with operating plans and standards, and to report and interpret the results of operations to all levels of management and to the owners of the business. This function includes the formulation of accounting policy, the coordination of systems and procedures, and the preparation of operating data and of special reports as required.

12. *Evaluating and Consulting:* To consult with all segments of management responsible for policy or action concerning any phase of the operation of the business as it relates to the attainment of objectives and the effectiveness of policies, organization structure and procedures

13. *Tax Administration:* To establish and administer tax policies and procedures

14. *Government Reporting*: To supervise or coordinate the preparation of reports to government agencies

15. *Protection of Assets:* To ensure protection for the assets of the business through internal control, internal auditing and the proper insurance coverage

16. *Economic Appraisal:* To appraise economic and social forces and government influences continuously, and to interpret their effect upon the business

Objectives for Controller Management Performance Measurement

17. Reduce clerical accounting costs by N dollars by installation of approved EDP by N date within capital budget of N dollars and expenses of N dollars.

18. Reduce monthly closing cycle by N days.

19. Reduce by N days the cycle time needed to prepare cost follow-up reports.

20. Reduce printing and copying costs by N dollars.

21. Hold auditing expense to no more than N dollars.

Controllership Management Plan of Action Elements

22. Review plans of operating departments to determine what service or support they will require.

23. Review departmental profit improvement opportunities.

24. Determine objectives.

25. Set plans for reaching objectives.

Monitors of Effectiveness of Financial Controls

26. Break-even point for product or project

27. Return on investment, overall and per product line.

28. Inventory costs, age, count and turnover

29. Cash and working capital liquidity, current and forecast

30. Current ratios:
- operating expenses to gross sales
- current assets to current liabilities
- cash liquidity compared to best competitors or industry averages
- capital expenditures to budget
- cost of sales to actual sales
- profit by unit and by product line
- actual sales to planned sales
- debt to equity

31. Variance analysis:
- expenses
- prices
- sales
- time
- product volume

- cash requirements
- gross profits
- per share earnings
- inventory
- budget performance
- per unit or product line profitability

32. Productivity:

- man-hours per production unit
- units produced per machine
- operating time in comparison with down time

33. Accounts receivable, turnover, age collection stats and "problem" accounts

34. Make-or-buy analysis and decisions

35. Working capital current ratios, loan restrictions, line of credit utilizations, lease obligations, temporary investment opportunities

36. Short- and long-range financial planning

37. Money market developments

38. Purchases vs. requirements

39. Discounts on purchases

Guidelines for Management in Budget Formulation

40. Budgets should be a control as well as a planning tool.

41. Budgets should measure performance by providing the basis for that measurement through specific and quantified plans.

42. Each manager should have clearly defined departmental objectives.

43. Plans and budgets should be prepared not only for departments, divisions, etc., but for overall corporate operations.

44. Variances from budgets are analyzed and variances corrected on an ongoing basis. Managers are called to task for continued deviations from planned budgets.

45. People who need to achieve specific, quantitative objectives are involved in the setting of the objectives. Responsibilities and standards are set.

46. The budgetary process is integrated within overall corporate planning.

47. Controllable and noncontrollable expenses as well as normal and abnormal expenditures are separated to account for planned deviations. Variable budgeting also indicates direct expenses for each item at its stage of production.

48. Specific review at specific periods, or when major changes in operations occur, allow for revising the budgets upward or downward.

49. Budgeting is a major managerial effort extending over a period of time. It is not only an important control tool for expenses and costs, but establishes standards and goals for the measurement of managerial performance.

50. Financial rewards and compensations are tied to performance goals.

Managerial Steps and Procedures in Formulating a Budget (See Figure 20-1)

51. The sales forecast is the beginning point, and it determines production, inventory levels and costs.

52. The production budget is calculated in the following manner:

Units to be produced = Planned ending inventory of
finished goods
plus (+)
planned sales
minus (−)
beginning inventory of
finished goods.

53. Material usage and purchases budget is determined: Purchases in units = desired ending material inventory quantities plus (+) usage minus (−) beginning inventory quantities.

54. Direct labor costs, factory overhead costs are determined next. These usually can be calculated from existing engineered data. Target inventory level is the inventory level at the end of the cycle.

55. Cost of goods sold budget is calculated.

56. Marketing, selling budget as well as general and administrative budgets, are factored into the master budget.

57. The cash budget provides an estimated effect on the cash position of the operations. Correctly used, it provides cash control and planning to avoid cash deficiences or surplus. The cash budget is factored with the cash receipts budget, which shows collections of receivables and other sources, as well as experience with bad debts and lag between sales and collections. Cash disbursements budget consists of material purchases averaging, outlays of direct labor wages, costs and expenses and disbursements such as purchases of fixed assets.

58. A pro forma balance sheet is thus reached.

Management Ratio Analysis for Corporate Financial Effectiveness

59. Net profit after tax divided by equity capital

60. Net profit before tax divided by total capital

61. Corporate tax divided by net profit before tax

62. Total profit divided by total capital

63. Interest paid divided by borrowed capital

64. Borrowed capital divided by equity capital (leverage measurement)

65. Total profit divided by interest paid

66. Total capital divided by borrowed capital

67. Current assets divided by current liabilities (quick ratio)

68. Stock divided by average daily cost of sales (stock turnover)

69. Debtors divided by average daily sales

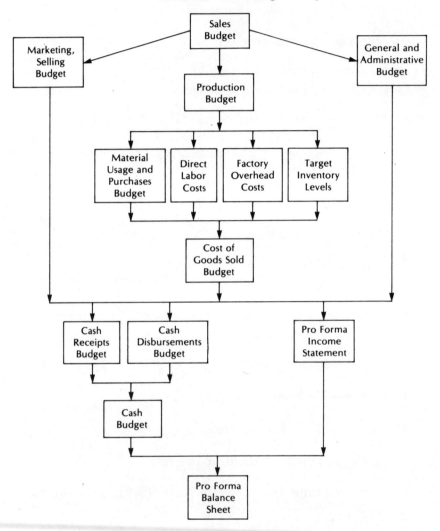

FIGURE 20-1
Financial Forecasting

70. Creditors divided by average daily purchases

71. Fixed expenditures divided by total expenditures (profit vulnerability)

72. Long-term capital divided by fixed assets

73. Income after tax divided by the value of the investment at the beginning of the period

74. Gross dividend receivable divided by the value of the investment at the beginning of the period

75. Capital gain divided by the value of the investment at the beginning of the period

76. Tax on dividend divided by gross dividend

77. Tax on gain divided by capital gains

78. Dividend (gross) divided by market value of ordinary shares

79. Profit after corporation tax divided by market value of ordinary shares

80. Market value of ordinary shares divided by profit after corporate tax

81. Profit after corporate tax divided by gross dividend

82. Profits after corporate tax divided by number of ordinary shares

83. Profit after corporate tax divided by equity capital

84. Net assets at book value divided by number of ordinary shares

85. Preference shares divided by total borrowed capital

86. Loans divided by total borrowed capital

87. Overdrafts divided by total borrowed capital

88. Trade and expense creditors divided by total borrowed capital

89. Corporate and/or income tax provisions divided by total borrowed capital

90. Income tax reserves and deferred taxation divided by total borrowed capital

91. Investment grants divided by total borrowed capital

92. Amount outstanding on hire purchase accounts divided by total borrowed capital

93. Amount outstanding on lease accounts divided by total borrowed capital

94. Debts factored divided by total borrowed capital

95. Bills discounted divided by total borrowed capital

Management Standards for Maintaining or Assessing Corporate Liquidity Status

96. Current ratio is a primary test which looks at assets available to pay liabilities falling due. It is calculated

$$\frac{\text{Current assets}}{\text{Current liabilities}}$$

(Normal "standards" are a two-to-one ratio.)

97. The quick ratio is a more selective standard. It concentrates on assets which can be turned quickly into cash, such as marketable securities and cash itself, but not stock:

$$\frac{\text{Quick assets}}{\text{Current liabilities}}$$

(Most managers hold that one-to-one is "standard" for most norms.)

98. Conventional ratios are backed up by "secondary" tests of liquidity, including:

- *Vulnerability of the company's profits during a slowdown of turnover (fixed costs/total costs).* In general, the higher this ratio the higher the company's ratio of current assets to current liabilities must be to survive any recession.
- *The speed at which the company is turning its stock over (stock/average daily costs of sales).* A rapid stock turnover will "excuse" a lower ratio of current assets to current liabilities.
- *Rapidity of debt collection (credits/average daily sales).* A fast debt collection will "explain" a low current asset to current liability ratio.
- *Credit amounts (credits/average daily purchases).* Higher rates than normal will tend to lower the ratio of current assets to current liabilities.

- *Long-term liabilities coming due in the near future.* The extent of these liabilities determines the current asset to current liability ratio that needs to be strengthened.
- *Capital expenditure plans.* Proposals for these plans will tend to run down the current asset to current liability ratio, unless there are immediate new plans also afoot to raise new finance soon.

99. Liquidity ratio calculation. This ratio calculates the effect rising inflation has on corporate liquidity:

$$\frac{\text{Stock plus debtors minus creditors}}{\text{Long-term capital}}$$

Monitors of Controllership Management Performance

100. Analyses of cost variances are routinely and regularly performed so that factors causing differences between standard and actual costs are identified and eliminated. Reports are printed and distributed.

101. Standards for variance analysis are based on engineered or other scientific data, rather than "historic" information.

102. Estimates for costs of a job or a process are within N percent of actual costs or time involved.

103. Variances are pinpointed as to material, labor or overhead variables in production areas.

104. Cost variances generate specific managerial action toward the accountable person as well as the accountable department.

105. Cost accounting systems apply to all departments of the company, including administrative and clerical areas.

106. Return on investment and other ratios are measured routinely on each project or product by line.

107. Cost control programs are prioritized.

108. Cost standards are no more than N months old; after reaching N months of use they are automatically out of date and must be replaced before use.

109. Cost control responsibility is shared by all employees, who are aware of these standards and goals.

110. Company employees who produce specific techniques to aid cost reduction through savings of time or material are rewarded in a company-wide program. Rewards are based on a task force's estimate of savings per year involved, and the employee is compensated on a percentage basis.

111. Budgets are set up for use at an appropriate user department level to show directly the interrelationship of the budget, actual costs and cost control reports:

- *Material usage reports* show not only material budgeted but a report of actual material used during a specific time span. Variance from standard is shown along with units produced and units budgeted to be produced.
- *Labor efficiency reports* show not only the direct labor actually used but the direct labor budgeted. Any change is shown in a "variance" column.
- *Overhead budget variance reports* show the budgeted costs and the actual costs and break out the variance.

112. Variable budgets show how each cost or expense will change with changes in volume or activity for each product or division of the company.

113. Cost controls are set prior to cost incurrence, rather than after cost incurrence, by providing supervisors with cost standards or objectives for scheduled work.

114. Cost controls are realistic, attainable and quantitative, and the people responsible for meeting controls have been actively involved in the planning process.

115. Cost controls are seen as positive factors, and employees have understanding of cost-consciousness.

116. Employees understand the standards involved, can measure cost controls by comparing actual costs with the standards set and thereby can gauge their own performance.

117. Cost control responsibilities have been affixed throughout the company. Each cost is the responsibility of some one individual, and he or she is held accountable.

118. Incurrence of cost is keyed to production activity.

119. Process costs systems, in which all costs are placed into "reservoirs" or "cost centers," have been investigated for usefulness and cost controls.

120. Determination has been made as to the best use of the LIFO or FIFO cost accounting system.

121. Standard costing systems, using set standards instead of attempting to determine an "actual" cost per unit in a period, is always double-checked with the use of variance analysis so that actual cost can be compared with predetermined costs and inefficiencies can be highlighted and eliminated.

122. Capital budgeting is an ongoing concern, not just "one shot."

123. Capital budgeting takes into account the timing of the cash flow through the use of present value methods.

124. Rate of return is calculated prior to a capital budgeting decision and return on investment is calculated after investment is undertaken to measure performance.

125. Mortgage financing, using the plant as collateral, has been investigated.

126. All borrowings are done by predetermined, systematic methods and are authorized by the board of directors.

127. Accounting is separated totally from other departments such as sales, purchasing, etc.

128. An internal auditor reports to a senior manager other than the controller.

129. Operating management reports are prepared to highlight variances as well as to report routine facts.

130. Major expenses and costs are under budgetary control.

131. Employees who work in ultra-sensitive areas are routinely rotated, and all employees are required to take full vacations.

132. Accounting manuals are in use, and books of account are kept up to date and are sufficient to the company's business.

133. Accounts receivable with customers are routinely confirmed by company personnel.

134. The credit department is independent of the sales department and operates on its predetermined standards for operations. These standards determine which companies will have credit. Credit performance is monitored so that operations suggest that all who meet standards have credit, and the bad debt ratio is not so low that it might suggest lost sales because of too-tight credit policies.

135. Employees who authorize credit do not have access to cash.

136. The credit department is consulted prior to the payment of a credit balance to a customer.

137. Customer accounts are balanced with control accounts by an employee specifically charged with this responsibility. He or she does not also handle the accounts receivable records.

138. Delinquent accounts are reviewed at stated frequencies by an accountable manager.

139. Trends of accounts receivable to days of sales are monitored closely for changes in aging.

140. Customers' orders of more than N dollars are subject to review and authorization prior to shipment.

141. Sales invoices are used. These are prenumbered, and all invoices are checked for accuracy.

142. Preparation of the company payroll is done within a system which involves a number of employees and which has a manager for final authorization and accountability.

143. Payroll accounts are reconciled every N days.

144. Investigations are made when unpaid employee checks are determined.

145. A separate manager is responsible for hearing employee grievances or questions about payroll checks or procedures.

146. All salary rates are in writing, along with any changes or additions. These have been signed by the appropriate managers or foremen.

147. Cash and currency are deposited daily in a bank account which pays interest.

148. A system for authenticating deposits as well as handling cash, particularly those coming in through the mail, is in use.

149. The bank has instructions not to cash checks made payable to the company but only to accept them for deposit. The bank has a list of only a few names of executives who can sign these checks for the company.

150. A policy has been developed for check cashing by employees.

151. Petty cash is handled by a system which restricts amounts and which controls responsibility for the money. Vouchers are used, books kept, and the funds are audited irregularly but often by an auditor independent of the fund or the department.

152. The ratio of costs of credit department, auditing department, etc., is calculated as a percentage of sales.

153. Inventory is closely monitored for levels, uses, costs and particularly timing. Cost records are tied to the financial records.

154. Inventory records are maintained no matter where in the plant material purchases are delivered. These records show the amount delivered and other pertinent checks. Discrepancies are immediately noted and action is taken.

155. Ratios for inventory have been calculated for best company use at various points in the company's production cycle. Purchasing's records are monitored to determine that purchases are neither more nor less, than what actually can be used during a predetermined period so that company investment in inventories is maintained at the lowest level possible.

156. Inventory records are checked against physical inventory every six months. Systematic checks to be made are detailed in written instructions.

157. An employee has the responsibility for maintaining controllership overviews on inventory, particularly if the company has large amounts of investment in this area.

158. Quantity, unit conversions, prices used, additions, extensions and summarizations are double-checked on inventory management.

Controllership Management Performance Objectives

159. Reduce fixed assets to a level not to exceed N percent of tangible net worth in N years.

160. Improve profits to gross sales from N percent to N percent within the next N months.

161. Reduce customer returned material from N dollars to N dollars within N months.

162. Reduce EDP costs by N percent within N months by elimination of N reports to be determined by value analysis and actual use.

163. Reduce the average age of accounts receivable from N days to N days.

164. Reduce bad debt losses to less than N percent of all sales.

165. Increase working cash by N percent in each of banks utilized within N months by limiting inventory levels to N percent of those currently carried.

166. Analyze expense trends five years out for each operating department based on the past five-year trends and set projected anticipated expenses. Then set a 10 percent reduction of those projected expense trends beginning with the first projected year.

167. Complete a cost manual and checklist and distribute this to each appropriate manager by N date.

Cost Accounting Management Checklist

168. Determinations of cost control responsibility

a. within the organization
b. organization of Comptroller's function
c. relationship with operating departments

169. Work authorization and flow checks

a. production requirements determination and order issuance procedures
b. material procurement determination (explosion) procedure (inventory
   check and open commitments procedure)
c. parts manufacturing determination and procedure (economic lot and
   inventory check and prior usage procedure)
d. factory scheduling and loading procedure (man-hour and equivalent
   man determination)
e. production control follow-up procedure
f. expediting procedure
g. inventory control on orders in process as related to new requirement
h. departmental flow and inspection points
i. inventory points
j. physical inventory situation
Note: Have work flow and authorization been charted?

170. Direct labor

a. basic direct labor defined (source by operation or by complete part?)
b. handling of auxiliary direct labor and inspection direct labor
c. method of arriving at direct labor standards and inclusion of items
   other than "pure" effort
d. plant and expense labor handling (burden application)
e. distinction between direct and indirect labor and reporting of diver-
   sions of direct labor
f. relationship of work standard to pay standard and effect on rate used
g. computation of work standard (used in cost standard)
h. computation of pay standard
i. (1) determination of rates used (use of standard rates or actuals dependent on feasibility)
   (2) base for recovery of burden from D/L (Standard hours, including
   rework, standard dollars, etc.)
j. flow of effort and identification with work standard (piece part) and
   operation or operator
k. scheduling and loading procedure

171. Direct material

a. identification of direct material—basic and auxiliary
b. costing of direct material and inclusions thereof (taxes, duties, incom-

ing transportation, insurance, packaging) and development of standard
c. price variance determination
d. plant and expense material
e. material burden inclusion
f. handling of special tooling charges
g. physical flow of material (flow checks) and paperwork support (requisitioning
    (1) receiving
    (2) raw material stores in and out
    (3) parts stores in and out
    (4) semifinished stores in and out
    (5) work in process in and out
    (6) finished goods in
h. issuance procedure of standard material (minimum issue, open requisitions, etc.) costing on requisition or standard B/M basis, excess material usage procedure and reporting as variance.

172. Shrinkage, rework, scrap, etc.

a. standards content for shrinkage, if any, and method used to determine contents (unavoidable engineered only)
b. method utilized to control excess shrinkage through control of material issues
c. handling of shrinkage in labor pay procedures
    (1) at operation discovered
    (2) on cost of prior operations
d. handling of rework
    (1) identification, responsibility determination
    (2) authorization for rework and paperwork procedure
    (3) costing of rework
    (4) use of standards in rework, where applicable, and where economically feasible
    (5) reporting
e. determination of scrap
    (1) identification of cost and responsibility
    (2) reporting against allowable shrinkage
    (3) physical handling and sale or reclaim procedures
f. production scrap applicability and costing
g.   physical handling and costing of customer returns

173. Packing and shipping costs

a. inclusion in manufacturing costs rather than sales and distribution costs
b. definition of direct labor and material in packing and shipping costs
c. handling of outgoing freight, cartage and insurance (terms of sale, etc.)
d. determination of Shipping Department burden and allocation to Assembly Departments in budget determination of burden rates
e. entries required

174. Manufacturing expense

a. item definitions
   (1) direct working
   (2) indirect working
   (3) indirect labor
b. use of associated labor benefits burden center
c. handling of maintenance expense (including purchased maintenance) and work order system
d. determination of manufacturing cost adjustments
e. definition of budget centers
f. definition of budget centers and number required
g. *annual* allocation only of service departments to production departments and bases used (for months use per day rather than 1/12) (no reallocation to other service department after initial allocation)
h. burden rate establishments
   (1) determination of normal practical capacity
   (2) manufacturing burden rates and base to be used (standard direct labor hours)
   (3) material burden rates and contents
i. flexible budgeting and application
   (1) definition of fixed (per work day) and variable (per hour) expenses (budget purposes only), emphasis on physical determinants (head count)
   (2) definition of unit of activity (standard labor hours, machine hours, etc.)
   (3) use of fixed and variable burden rates in studies and variance determination only
   (4) use of indirect manning tables and other physical unit planning documents
   (5) issuance of budget reports prior to the start of a period.

175. Entries

a. cost inputs

b. cost outputs
    (1) standard costs to inventory
    (2) transfers to assets
    (3) plant and expense control balances
    (4) variances, cost adjustments, and their computations (including material burden variances)
c. adjustments to actual costs, where requied
d. costing of sales procedures

176. Paperwork flow

a. purchase, receipt, inspection and storage of and payment for purchased material
b. material issuance
c. recording of direct labor and costing and distribution
d. work order system for maintenance, etc.
e. cost accounting procedures relative to above inputs, cost output, control reports and handling of data

177. Standards revisions

a. present procedures, approvals, and causes (when made: annually or during year)
b. identification of parts in all products on which used (used on file)
c. (1) effect on inventory and valuation
    (2) cost of modification and handling
d. entries used
e. profit implications and their handling

178. Reports

a. departmental control reports by budget center
    (1) off-standard performance labor and material
    (2) direct working
    (3) indirect labor
    (4) rework
    (5) scrap and shrinkage
    (6) manufacturing expenses
    (7) variance reports and analyses
    (8) summary report of variances, rework and other controllable costs
b. segregation of controllable vs. noncontrollable with *all* cost accounted for

179. Pricing

a. comptroller's activity responsibility for a review of sales prices for reasonableness, inclusion of all cost elements, and desirability from the profit and financial viewpoint (standard margin report with sales at catalog price and actual billed price)
b. control of inventory cost through:
   (1) valuation control (at standard)
   (2) usage control through reporting of inventory level vs. usage

180. Implementation schedule

a. steps (including flow chart requirements)
b. time schedule
c. responsibility

21

HOW TO MEASURE EDP/MIS MANAGEMENT PERFORMANCE

Background Data for Management

1. Have your data processing and managerial information systems been designed from the top down, with your top departmental managers actively deciding what data will be used?

2. When was the last time you had an EDP audit? Was it within the last year?

3. Is the cost ratio of EDP/MIS rising faster than you would like? What "standards" for cost comparison and control do you use?

4. Do your EDP systems report on *all* main functions of the company, or do they primarily revolve around sales and financial data? Are they used to monitor management performance as expressed by key ratios?

5. Are EDP/MIS processing services charged back to user departments? Who are the main users? Is this service "in balance" with actual management needs?

6. When was the last time you checked the actual value and the use made of the information generated from EDP? Have you identified and substantially cut back on less valuable information?

7. Are security systems in effect so that EDP employees have specialized and controlled job functions and limited EDP access to prevent "computer theft?"

Ratios to Measure and Monitor EDP/MIS Management Performance

8. Data processing costs divided by sales

9. Data processing costs divided by transactions (Transactions are the total of all purchases, payments, sales receipts, etc. entering the EDP system.)

10. EDP transactions divided by sales

11. Value of reports to management divided by the cost of producing them (The latter attempts to place a monetary value on reports which management and departments request and involves EDP and department costs. This "value" then can be used to evaluate the actual usefulness of the report, or aspects of the report, to management.)

Method of Ranking EDP/MIS Reports for Report "Pruning"

12. Not all reports are equally useful to management and departments. To evaluate reports periodically, which is necessary since reports seem to grow "like Topsy," a system of ranking is needed.

One useful ranking technique is the "paired comparison." Each manager is surveyed to compare a "pair" of reports and to decide which is the better report. The surveying sequence, and the awarding of ranking points:

- *Is report X more useful than report Y?* (If so, then report X is awarded 2 points.)
- *Is report Y more useful than report X?* (If so, then report Y is awarded 2 points.)
- *Are reports X and Y of equal value?* (If so, then each is awarded 1 point.) However, this essential "lack of decision" making is to be avoided, if possible, through the use of further decision-evoking questions such as:

    a. Which report did you last spend the most time with?
    b. Which report do you rely upon for your major decisions?
    c. If you had to do without one report, which one would that be?

From this sequence of questions, most managers will arrive at a relative, comparative value of informational data or reports.
Note: The same value ranking system can be applied to specific items, ratios, percentages, sums and even variances to determine the most and the least valuable data contained in a report.

13. The information is displayed in the Value Ranking Chart, with the vertical axis representing the numerical sum of points awarded, and the horizontal axis displaying the costs. The graph is then divided into three bands of information labeled Band A, Band B, and Band C.

14. Analysis of the value ranking bands:
Band A: The top band identifies high-value, low-cost data. This band
is the top priority for managerial continuance.
Band B: The middle band identifies middle-value, moderate-cost
data (with some data extending in value to the upper portions of the scale). The data, particularly those falling into

VALUE RANKING

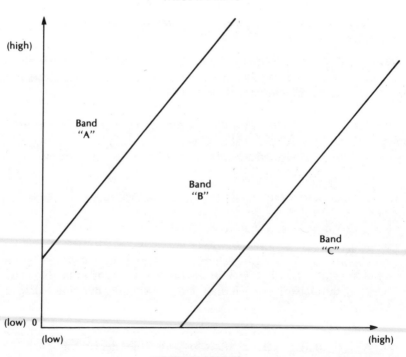

COSTS OF REPORT

the lower ranges, should be questioned in depth, and portions of the data should be discontinued.

Band C: The lower band identifies data which are comparatively high in cost and low in value. Most of these reports should be discontinued or substantially modified.

EDP/MIS Management Criteria for Control Report Design

15. What types of management decisions will be made from the EDP/MIS-provided data or report?

16. Who will be using the report, and to what degree will this person rely on the data to make a decision?

17. What detail should be presented? Should the report or data encapsulate key items or should key items and background analysis be presented? What amount of background is most useful?

18. What is the best form in which to display the data? Are graphs or comparative visual devices useful to show relationships between or among data, deviations or variations from standard data, time, weight, amount measurement or trends?

19. How much time should a manager spend on the report? Should the key thought, or recommendations, be grasped in just a few minutes?

20. Should the reporting data be prioritized, with the most important information at the top and less important information displayed in descending order?

21. If the report is to be a "Decision Document," then should the recommendation be handled concisely on a separate cover page and all supporting documents attached to this page?

22. Is the report designed specifically to meet the needs of decision makers as well as the needs of the situation, in both form and content

23. Is the report clear, accurate, concise, readable and timely? Can it, in and by itself, be relied upon?

Management Control Information: Generation and End Usages

24. Input of financial or budget data, such as current liabilities, current assets, etc., is calculated by EDP/MIS as management ratios for trends analysis as well as standards for ongoing control reports.

25. Input of sales targets by product line, sales forecasting or sales expenses by various categories is calculated to be used as ongoing control reports to monitor objectives as well as management ratios.

26. Inventory levels and other data, including stock and raw materials, as well as inventory pricing standards, are calculated for each plant's management with resultant control reports and other data on stock and expenses.

27. Production inputs, including material, labor and overhead expenses, are calculated to arrive at costs as well as productive standards and other control reports for management.

28. Production inputs including work orders, schedules, timetables, machine speeds, materials, manpower and records, are calculated to arrive at total requirements for labor, for materials, and schedules to be adhered to in the form of work orders for production, delivery instructions and schedules as well as, finally, purchase orders for new inventory to replace that used.

29. Production inputs, including directions for manpower, production rates, machine usages, speeds, etc., are calculated to determine tooling requirements, plant loadings and actual outputs with accompanying data for determinations of productivity and other management performance ratios.

30. Manpower use inputs, including paid time, incentive plan allowance, wage rates, overtime, etc., are calculated to determine actual and projected manpower costs against standards, payroll data, budget figures and management control reports and performance ratios.

31. Nonproductive time inputs, such as "down" time on machines due to machinery failure or routine maintenance, are calculated for management control reports, planning and analysis.

32. Stock item-raw material usage, including inputs from material use records, yield records, waste records, etc., are calculated by EDP/MIS to determine stock requirements, to figure material yields and to update inventory records. These data also result in outputs for purchase orders, stock renewals and management control reporting effectiveness of material use.

33. Inputs on suppliers invoices, purchase requisitions, cancellation, etc., are calculated for processing of accounts and purchase orders, and to generate continuing reports on supplier performance.

Monitors to Measure EDP/MIS Management Performance to Objectives

34. EDP/MIS is used to report on all major aspects of the company's operation, including sales analysis, production control, cash flow analysis, financial modeling, marketing analysis and purchasing.

35. EDP/MIS increases decision-making information, including management performance and other ratios, at the rate of N percent a year.

36. The output generated is reliable for decision making, is pertinent and is accurate.

37. EDP/MIS output meets the needs of the management teams it serves, through the use of surveys each N months.

38. EDP/MIS output contains less than N percent errors in relationship to total output.

39. The department has been audited within the last six months to monitor EDP/MIS:

- quality and cost performance
- organization and staffing
- system design effectiveness
- input preparation
- format and effectiveness of output
- machine utilization efficiency and effectiveness
- security
- improvement possibilities and needs
- controls and planning
- documentation
- installation and physical plant
- reporting procedures and project progress
- training of MIS/EDP personnel and work standards
- library and storage systems
- processing and programming effectiveness

40. EDP/MIS has, within the last six months, conducted a check on the usefulness of the items of data generated through the use of the value ranking techniques.

41. Data identified as both of minor importance and higher-than-average in cost have been analyzed.

42. Costs of EDP/MIS have been calculated in terms of sales as well as transactions and the ratios are monitored for performance and effectiveness.

43. EDP/MIS costs have not varied more than 5 per cent from budgeted amounts each year.

44. Major suppliers of EDP equipment have inputs into the department so that the company's operation is constantly measured against the latest applicable technology.

45. Economic justification studies have been made within the last six months to lease, lease-buy, or buy EDP equipment for future needs.

46. Adequacy of the system has been analyzed within the last year for current needs as well as the company needs one year out, two years out and four years out.

47. EDP/MIS is able to attract high-quality personnel to handle its operations effectively and well.

48. Studies have been completed on the use of human resource stimulating programs such as flex time, task teams, accountability centers and various reward systems to enhance performance. One of these systems is now used within the department and the system's performance, in turn, is being analyzed.

49. The department has a table of organization, with job descriptions and responsibilities. Each employee has been trained in his or her particular job and can meet written standards. Moreover, to provide "depth" to the operation, key employees have been given training in different procedures and jobs.

50. Written standards and objectives exist for each job.

51. Documentation is complete for each program and is maintained after each run. It includes the flow chart, coding sheets, appropriate controls used, the printout form, layouts, complete instructions and the names of the key persons accountable for the job.

52. Operations schedules are published in advance and contain appropriate and complete planning data as well as responsibilities.

53. Machine log times are maintained and show production time, rerun time, maintenance time and down time.

54. Management analyzes use of machines, including their productivity and hours run, to determine the need for replacement equipment and to make decisions on rent-or-buy.

55. Records are maintained and analyzed on run errors, reruns and machine or programming failures to spot trends and eliminate future problems.

56. Security measures over EDP/MIS include locked doors, authorized areas for EDP/MIS personnel only, badges to identify people in areas, controls over programs, inputs and equipment, and limits on the responsibility and the authority any one person bears during any operation.

57. Security procedures and policies prevent tampering with records or programming which might allow "computer theft."

58. Requests for processing or special processing are handled only on the basis of written and authorized documents.

59. Financial forms, such as checks, are sequentially numbered and accounted for.

60. All important tape disks are stored in a fire-safe, locked area away from the processing center to safeguard the data.

61. Controls prevent unauthorized changes or tampering with important tape-disk packs.

62. A backup computer system is available in case of a breakdown or other problem.

63. EDP/MIS costs for reports or data are charged back to requesting departments, and these departments are accountable for costs.

64. Reports are analyzed each six months on the departmental use of EDP/MIS as well as the number of reports and the time needed to generate them. Top management determines what percent of EDP/MIS is being utilized for specific purposes and makes a value judgment on this use's overall significance within the company structure.

65. EDP/MIS conducts a regular training program to manager-trainees on the management use and capabilities of computers. Included is an understanding of how a computer can serve the needs of the management, as well as applications of computer-generated management reports and performance or measurement ratios.

22

HOW TO MEASURE
PERSONNEL MANAGEMENT
PERFORMANCE

Background Data for Management

1. Has your organization formally clarified what kind of "people skills" make a difference to your business?

2. Is an active effort made to find and support people who have these skills?

3. Does personnel management actively move into day-to-day administration activities throughout the company? Or does personnel management follow a mode of predicting problems before they occur, discussing them after they occur, but doing little which actually impacts a solution to problems when they actually occur?

4. Does the company have an open and direct environment, or is it all too much tied to the rigidity of the organization chart?

5. Is Personnel management responsible not only for finding and selecting candidates but for retaining them?

6. Are employees held accountable for accomplishing specific results rather than simply for doing activities? Are job responsibilities clearly delineated in terms of results or objectives? Is there a close and objective monitoring process in which both supervisor and employee participate and both know the rules and the score?

7. Are training and management development programs keyed to results-oriented performance? Are they designed and delivered by professionals?

8. Does the company have a "manpower data bank" in which accurate and comprehensive data about all personnel performance are stored? Is the "bank" continuously monitored, and does each managerial file contain the latest performance appraisal data, job-related strengths and weaknesses, and individual development plan, probable career moves and future potential? Is it used to select candidates for promotion?

9. Do some departments seem to have "traditional" problems with absenteeism or high rates of turnover?

10. What is your company's productivity ratio? Can this productivity be enhanced through greater emphasis on developing the company's human resources, at a minimal cost?

11. Do other executives regard personnel management as hard-hitting, no-nonsense managers with wide-ranging impact on the organization?

12. Do you have a management replacement plan projected for the next two years? The next five?

13. Are managers throughout the company reviewed regularly for progress and especially for signs of "middlescence," "midlife crisis," or other signs of work slowdown or career arrest? What programs do you have designed to make these persons productive once again? How effective have they actually been?

Sample Objectives to Measure Personnel Management Performance

14. Reduce recruiting costs by N dollars or N percent.

15. Formulate approved incentive system by N date for X department to increase productivity by N percent or decrease costs by N percent.

16. Maintain cafeteria costs at N dollars per month without loss of food quality.

Personnel Management Plan of Action Elements

17. Review of plans of operating departments to determine what service or support they will require

18. Review of departmental profit improvement opportunities

19. Setting objectives

20. Formulating plans for reaching objectives.

Personnel Management Performance Enhancement Considerations

21. Using recruiting consultants versus internal recruiters

22. Using outside versus inside testing

23. Operating the employee cafeteria versus turning it over to a concession operator

24. Paying personnel on an hourly basis versus an incentive basis

25. Weighing effectiveness of written communications versus personal briefing sessions by supervisors

26. Using on-the-job training versus vestibule training

27. Using in-company versus university management development activities

28. Choosing between manual preparation and maintenance of personnel records versus the use of EDP

29. If nonunion, what is the cost/benefit tradeoff of continuing nonunion versus going union?

Ratio of Measurement for Personnel Management Effectiveness

30. Personnel costs divided by average number of employees

31. Recruiting costs divided by number of recruits retained

32. Training costs divided by average number of employees

33. Costs of wage increases in excess of industry standards divided by average number of employees

34. Cost of lost production attributed to industrial relations problems divided by average number of employees

35. Number of man-days which were lost, divided by number of man-days worked

36. Number of man-days lost through absenteeism divided by number of man-days worked.

37. Number of employees who leave divided by average number of employees

38. Number of employees with one year of service divided by number of people employed a year ago

39. Number of employees with more than one year of service divided by total employed

40. Training costs divided by training days

41. Training days divided by trainees

42. Trainees divided by total employees

43. Recruiting costs divided by recruits interviewed

44. Recruits selected divided by recruits interviewd

45. Number of recruits accepting employement divided by recruits selected

46. Number of recruits who remain on job more than twelve months divided by number of recruits who accepted employment

Areas of Personnel Management Measurement of Management and Employees

47. Productivity rate of company (compared with rate of leading competitor of industry)

48. Individual performance shown during special work on "task teams"

49. Data in EDP manpower library

50. Performance appraisals

51. Identification of job-related strengths and weaknesses by supervisors and management

52. Promotions, accomplishements and overall "track record" of results

53. Training or educational classes completed along with final "grade" or evaluation

54. Career moves and individual development plans

55. Individually expressed priorities

56. Return on investment and profit generation

57. Management ranking as a "cost center"

58. Time lost or productivity lost

59. Absences

60. Accident frequency or severity

61. Size of employee work force

62. Number of supervisors and management to size of work force

63. Distribution of work force by training, by experience, by age and by education

64. Intercompany work force mobility and promotion rate

65. Number of "outside specialists" hired for key positions or in lieu of promoting current employees

66. Strike frequency, duration and severity

67. Results produced by strikes or slowdowns or other employee unrest

68. Arbitration costs

69. Benefit costs as a percent of compensation

70. Personnel requirements

71. Recruitment and training costs

72. Retirement forecasts and percentages of work force

73. Work force turnover percentage

74. Results achieved by training as measured in quantifiable, objective testing

75. Percentage of implementation of performance appraisal recommendations

76. Percentage of objectives actually accomplished compared with those agreed to

77. Understanding of employees about the nature of the company, its competitive status, products, markets, standards and objectives

78. Achievement of individual standards and goals

79. Health problem rates and profile trends

80. Percentage of error

81. Percentage of overtime costs and trends

82. Employee suggestions submitted, percentage accepted, and awards given

83. Requests for transfer

84. Cost ratios for employee advertising, recruitment and selection

85. Costs of testing applicants

86. Ratios for settlement of grievances as well as frequencies and trends

87. Separation analysis

88. Tardiness

89. Break-even performance

90. Performance in maintaining budget costs and deadlines

91. Number of customer complaints

92. Dividend record

93. Cash flow and liquidity

94. Facilities and machine utilization

95. Materials, stock and other expenses

96. Amount of "yield" produced compared with raw materials used

97. Methods and time-and-motion studies

98. New products developed, new ideas attempted, number of patents acquired or applied for

99. Number of sales calls made per sales person and individual sales-person productivity

100. Sales expense per individual, per territory or per product line

101. Sales skills of sales people as quantified in objective testing

102. Conformance to environmental, special interest, and other groups' expressed needs

103. Work sampling and testing against standards and objectives

104. Bonus amounts and percentages

105. Incentive plan performance and measurement

106. Stock bonus and other options

107. Compensation rates and trends

108. Contract negotiations and results

109. Number of hours spent in management training

110. Amount of savings achieved through employee suggestions or in-novations

111. Ratio of employees available for promotions compared to total employees

112. Services provided to customers compared with total possible serv-ices

113. Measurements of attitudinal dynamics of employees

114. Leadership in professional, business, civic or educational institutions or organizations

Key Psychological, Sociological and Other Needs Analysis as Elements of Employee Motivation for Managers

Each employee, for optimum performance, needs
115. Supportive environment in which to work

116. To know periodically where he or she stands in performance of job

117. Training to learn exactly what results (not activities) are to be achieved on the job

118. Understanding of job standards to be able to measure for himself or herself how well he or she is doing

119. To feel he or she is growing within the company and that this growth will make the future secure

120. A feeling of being needed, that people will listen when important, and that his or her energies, ideas and work are not only heard but are of interest to management

121. To feel the company offers him or her security and protection against uncertainties of life through insurance benefits and, ultimately, retirement with pension

122. To have inputs into the work he or she does and the feeling that the extra effort or "caring" expended is appreciated and will be rewarded

123. To feel he or she is an "expert" at doing his or her own job

124. To be heard when he or she is annoyed, bothered or frustrated by work which is too simple, routine or boring or, on the other hand, too complex or difficult

125. To feel he or she has an opportunity to grow as much as he or she can grow and thus find his or her own level in the organization

126. Orientation, training and supervisor guidance to feel comfortable in his or her specialized job and to find interest and challenge in it

127. To feel management and the company are dealing fairly with him or her in wages earned, in work to be completed, in standards set and in pay scales in relation to other companies

128. Supportive coaching to use procedures or methods not used often

129. To feel his or her education, personal and professional, continues with work in the organization, and does not end with high school or college

130. To feel he or she is a valued member of the organizational "team" and has good communications and inputs as a member in good standing

131. To feel he or she is earning advances in salary based on extra effort or output, that the company rewards this extra effort quickly and with gratitude

132. Direct feedback from his or her supervisor or manager to determine how well the company ranks his or her performance against standards, and, moreover, receives specific coaching to do better

133. Recognition for his or her effort, so as to have some identity within the group or within the community

134. To feel worthwhile in the organization and to have direct involvement in setting standards he or she is expected to accomplish

135. To feel that the company is progressing and that he or she is progressing with the company

136. To feel that change is the inevitable result of growth and that growth, and thus change, is generally beneficial

137. To know his or her place within the group and the group's position within the organization; to have the flexibility to move from group to group as new and more challenging positions become available

138. To feel a respected member of the organization, with important individual strengths and with specific contributions to be made

139. To feel his or her potential is recognized and encouraged by management

140. To feel always that he or she is being treated as an "adult" and a competent "individual"

Monitoring Standards of Personnal Management

141. All jobs within the company have been described and classified within the last two years.

142. Key entry jobs are analyzed to determine exact and "real world" basic functions. These data are used to determine realistic job qualifications so that applicants are screened to meet the *actual* needs of the job.

143. Personnel monitors the company work force through EDP, including qualifications of the "manpower library" to determine advancements based on skills, job experience and company track record.

144. Personnel levels, expenses, turnover (particularly by department), injury, absenteeism, recruiting performance, training costs, and ratios of performance, etc., are carefully monitored, trends noted and acted upon.

145. Personnel has developed a five-year management replacement plan whereby positions within the company, such as president, executive staff, general staff, etc. are identified as to number of positions, vacancies, retirements, or early retirements so as to determine the total number of promotions needed up the managerial pyramid. From this chart, Personnel determines how many new top executives will be needed, how many department managers, how many middle managers, and how many new people are to be hired and retained to begin grooming for management-level positions.

146. Job standards for each position have been developed, and an applicant knows and understands what is expected, based on these data prior to hiring.

147. Applicants are screened to meet the actual needs of the job, to be able to perform work to meet job standards, and to meet minimum needs. They are not overqualified nor better skilled than needed to meet standards and minimum needs.

148. Pay scales for all employee categories are reviewed by compensation specialists so that employees' pay, overtime, and benefits are in line with current trends and meet competition.

149. Standards are in effect for hiring new employees. An applicant's past records with other companies are checked, individual tests are completed, and, the manager who will be accountable for the employee's performance will have input into the hiring process.

150. All new employees receive an orientation on the company, how it operates, what its goals and objectives are, how the work force is managed, what work standards are as well as company personnel policies, procedures and benefits. This orientation is accomplished through the issuance of a corporate employee "handbook" to the employee after he or she is hired, but prior to the employee's starting work. A brief written "quiz" at the end of the handbook is to be filled out by the employee and submitted to the supervisor, who then reviews the "answers" to be certain the employee has correct orientation, information and assumptions about the company.

151. New employees receive a copy of individual job standards, which stress results to be accomplished rather than activities.

152. Each new employee receives a personal orientation by his or her supervisor on the department, the work performed by the department and the objectives and standards of the department, the "accountability" system of the department to other departments, the company, and to customers. The methods by which the individuals, and the department are rated, including regular reviews of performance and feedback on *both* strengths and weaknesses, are detailed along with specific information on earning more pay tied to performance.

153. Regular reviews of performance against standards occur each six months in such a manner that each new employee and his or her supervisor know, openly and realistically, what has been done, what's right and what's wrong, where each stands and, most important, what needs to be done to improve performance.

154. Supervisors and managers are trained extensively in management techniques for good manpower utilization. These techniques include: basic insights into human motivation, basic "needs of employees," methods of behavioral "reinforcements," as well as how to conduct interviews, how to rate employee performance, how to conduct open, professional and frank performance appraisals as well as separate counseling sessions to minimize weaknesses and maximize strengths of individuals.

155. Adequate training programs are carried on to meet the needs of skills levels for employees as well as management and performance data for supervisors and management.

156. Management development training is based on the needs of management, enhances company performance goals and is presented by competent professional trainers.

157. When managers or staff attend an outside training program, they bring back an assessment of the effectiveness of the program, the practicality of the material and the professionalism of the trainer. Personnel maintains a file on the preferred training programs and makes an assessment of their worth as demonstrated by the attendee. Inadequate, poorly structured or delivered, or primarily esoteric programs are identified, and no more personnel are scheduled to attend.

158. A library of business, professional and technical books, tapes and audio manuals is maintained for the benefit of those who wish to utilize this information for home study.

159. Exceptional information, such as books of outstanding interest, professional articles of pertinence or classes of more than routine impact, are summarized in written brief form, and this information is duplicated and made available for home study.

160. Personnel management is actively concerned with the daily operating activities of the company and their impact upon the overall management of the human resource and its performance.

161. Personnel is responsible for the retention as well as the selection of employees. It aids in determining the total requirements of jobs when an employee is to be promoted and in deciding on whether the employee has the capabilities for the job, including skills, duties, reporting interrelationship, responsibilities, authorities, standards, objectives and planning so that the right people are always being groomed for the right management position. Personnel monitors individual career progress.

162. The track record of individual work on each "task team" is monitored since this will allow Personnel to determine individual manager's ability prior to being placed in a line or staff responsibility.

163. A "systems approach" to management is promoted so that the focus of the work is on achieving specific results.

164. Standards for open and honest communications are set by top management and reinforced by Personnel communications, including corporate newsletters, memos or employee bulletins. Such communications talk "real world" facts about the company, sales or markets, corporate developments, personnel changes and problem solving. They are intended to keep an employee abreast of what he or she actually needs to know about the company and the company's progress and problems.

165. All legal requirements for hiring and employment, including minorities and women. are being observed and monitored.

166. Checks are made periodically to be certain that employees are receiving the skills and professional training they need to meet standards.

167. A supervisor's handbook details methods of handling problems common to all supervisors and includes conducting interviews legally and correctly, handling appraisals, methods of systematizing potential discipline problems, handling grievances, dealing with problems in a systematic manner and how to maintain open, two-way communications with employees.

168. Employees are encouraged to make suggestions which will benefit the company's efficiency, profitability or productivity. Rewards for suggestions are quickly given, based on a "task team's" prompt evaluations.

169. Objectives for the Personnel Department are set with the aid of personnel management, which is called to answer for meeting objectives or to determine why objectives have not been met. Rewards are tied to outstanding accomplishment of objectives.

23

A Final Note . . . PEOPLE!

Dear reader, you deserve sincere and large congratulations! You have succeeded in completing a book that must seem as intriguing as a dictionary or, more accurately, a cookbook. Yet I feel that I must call upon you to weather just a bit more, because all will have been for naught if you have become *so* enmeshed with the "How To" that you fail to remember to give prime attention to the "What For"!

In *No-Nonsense Management* I tried to make managers aware of the *need* for measurement of managerial performance. Rather than presenting deathless prose here, I leave to you the untarnished joy of initial reading. In this companion book, I have provided you with a "running *start*" toward a practical approach to actually measuring managerial performance.

The quantitative, objective and impersonal "No-Nonsense Management" approach has been misunderstood by some to lack "humanity," to fail to take the "human factor" into account. The simple truth is, of course, that the "No-Nonsense Management" approach, with its *demand* for continual professional and personal improvement, is indeed far more "humane" than subjective, qualitative "paternalism" which, under the noble and high-sounding banner of "humanism," actually emasculates individualism and demeans professional individual dignity. "Humanism" too often cloaks mundane meddling.

The "paternalistic" or "personal" approach results only in giving fish to the hungry; while the "No-Nonsense Management" approach, rather, teaches the hungry how to catch their own fish. Goethe was not known as a management philosopher, but he captured the very essence of "No-Nonsense Management" when he said:

> Treat people as if they were what they *ought to be* and you help them to
> become what they are capable of being.

The notion of "ought to be" is NOT new, really, to business management. It is, after all, at the core of any standard cost system. So, all I expect of you is to take that concept out of the "accounting closet," bring it into the searing light of the boardroom and make it the keystone of your managerial interrelationships.

As you proceed to implement the "No-Nonsense Management" approach, do NOT fail to remember that you are, after all, dealing with *PEOPLE*; not collectively, but individually. As individuals they each have their own motivational "hot button," their own "whatever it is that turns you on." There is *NO* requirement of effective general managership which states, "You must be a practicing psychologist." It is simply not a prerequisite to effective general managership that you understand the answer to the question, "*Why* did so-and-so do (or say) such-and-such?" Far too many valuable hours are wasted on endless speculation.

Be content only to know that "so-and-so *actually did* (or said) such-and-such!" And treat with the reality of it all.

Be aware that the PEOPLE with whom you are concerned can be classified; and, further, that the measure of your effectiveness is in direct proportion to your ability to treat with them in a class-selective manner. The notion is not totally dissimilar to a "stratification of the market" approach. A "No-Nonsense" approach must, after all, be "sold." People simply do not rush to the embrace of accountability and vulnerability.

The most important class is, of course, the OWNERS. They come in varying shades of interest and motivation. As a professional manager-employee (a "hired hand"), the sure-fire initial approach, absent preference to the contrary, is to take those steps which "enhance the enduring value of the shareholder investment." Your objective is, simply, to make the shareholders, the owners, wealthy (wealthier)! Proceed on the premise that they want to receive the *maximum* return on their investment.

Sometimes you will encounter owners who really do not want to receive the maximum return in terms of dollars! It's not all that unthinkable. First of all, owners (*true* entrepreneurs, that is) rarely think of themselves as being in the "this or that product/industry business"; rather, they view themselves as in the "investment" business. They have entrusted some of their dollars to you, as a professional manager, to earn money for them. Earn how much money? Well, that depends. Some owners are willing to forgo a portion of dollar return because they obtain gratification from playing "Santa Claus"—e.g., by paying discretionary "Christmas bonuses," by paying higher wages and salaries to employees than is competitively necessary, by providing working conditions more comfortable than legally or functionally required, by, in other words, being (or trying to be) a "good egg."

In short, they gratify a need (it's not important *why* they have that need) to "meddle" in personal lives. They exaggerate and overreach their position. They confuse legal rights of ownership with social rights of feudal lordship which have, long ago, been rejected by true individualists. Or they may be truly genuine altruists.

The gratification thus obtained is otherwise known as "psychic income." The sum of dollar income and psychic income is always equal to the optimum dollar return obtainable by alternative investment. In other words, the amount of psychic income that an owner enjoys can be measured precisely as the gap of dollar income that exists between dollar income received and the maximum return obtainable from alternative investment.

Again, absent direction (either explicit or implicit) to the contrary, your prime obligation to the most important class of people with whom you will deal is to maximize return on the owners' investment. Once you really understand that and make it an integral and foundational keystone to the exercise of management, implementing with "No-Nonsense" will follow as a matter of course. And, you will find it's a lot easier on you and your subordinates, too!

No longer need you be plagued with the anxiety of trying to recognize the "effort" which subordinates put forth; no longer will you waste priceless hours pondering the "why" of actions/words of subordinates; no longer will you confuse "experience" with mere tenure; no longer need you bear the burden of "playing God" with people's lives.

The second classification of PEOPLE with whom you will deal are employees-officers, managers, supervisors and "doers." Your primary obligation to them is to provide an environment for opportunity for professional growth and development.

In turn, there are two subclasses. First, there is the group (numerically in a very small minority) of individualists who truly desire to grow professionally and have a deep, genuine interest in their chosen profession of business management. This is the group that we are vitally interested in, because they represent our undeniably most valuable resource. I'll have more to say of them a little later.

Second, the largest group in American business is composed of people who, really, have no abiding interest in either their work or their employer. Too often, they mask their managerial inadequacies with the self-serving facade, "My family comes first." And yet, upon inspection, the tragic findings reveal that they perform their familial duties with equally mediocre verve and commitment.

Nonetheless, the facet of their lives with which we are here concerned is bounded by "normal working hours." Security, in their terms, means job security; inner assurance that they will "always" be able to arrive, "do their thing" and depart without involvement, commitment or vulnerability.

Your task as an effective manager is, somehow, to meet the needs of both subclasses. Happily, there is a way, but only one way—the "No-Nonsense" way! A firm which records a growth pattern of healthy, high-quality profitability not only provides the one and only means to meet the needs of both the "tigers" and the "pussycats" but—Eureka!—also meets the demands of investor-owners.

The security-seekers need look no farther. Their jobs are indeed secure! The tigers will be able to extend their "territorial integrity" to the limits only of their own individual creative aggressiveness. And, most important, the owners will have maximized their return!

Now, back to my favorite people—the tigers! Generally, the "best" managerial candidates are those who display "inordinate acquisitiveness" or, more simply, GREED. They want to *earn* more money; they don't want their earning potential limited or controlled in ANY way other than their own *performance.*

A "No-Nonsense Management" approach provides the means to gratify their greed. After "stretch" objectives have been identified, a "no-ceiling" Incentive Compensation Plan will provide for incremental compensation directly and impersonally related to incremental performance. Among your most challenging tasks is to so define the array of objectives that personal, greedy performance will result in compellingly attractive return to the investor-owners. The objectives, tier by tier, must be mutually supportive of and consistent with the objectives of the entire firm—a pyramid, if you will, culminating in "return on investment" at the apex.

The inferences regarding management style (whatever that is) are inescapable. When "No-Nonsense" objectives are teamed with incentive compensation and adequate financial controls, and all are, in turn, coupled with a "tiger" organization, the most effective approach that you, as a general manager, can take is:

> EITHER LEAD,
> FOLLOW
> OR
> GET THE HELL OUT OF THE WAY!!

INDEX